Jockeys of the Seventies

Jockeys of the Seventies

Tim Fitzgeorge-Parker

LONDON
Pelham Books

First published in Great Britain by
Pelham Books Ltd
44 Bedford Square
London WC1
1980

©1980 by Tim Fitzgeorge-Parker

British Library Cataloguing in Publication Data

Fitzgeorge-Parker, Tim
    Jockeys of the seventies.
    1. Horse-racing — Great Britain — History —
    20th century
    2. Jockeys — Great Britain
    3. Steeplechasing — Great Britain — History —
    20th century
    I. Title
    798 ' .43 '0922   SF335.G7

ISBN 0 7207 1267 X

Typeset by Cambrian Typesetters Ltd.
Printed and bound by Billing and Sons Ltd,
Guildford and Worcester

The photographs in this book are by courtesy of
Sport and General Press Agency.

Contents

Acknowledgements

I wish to acknowledge the help and co-operation of the jockeys in compiling this book; my special thanks go to Lester Piggott. I am also indebted to the *Daily Mail* without whose employment I would have been unable to gather so much of the material.

Tim Fitzgeorge-Parker

Introduction

Jockeys of the seventies without Lester Piggott would be like *Hamlet* without the Prince. So, in painting the scene, I have found it necessary to leave in the forefront the three stars, who were in their prime during this decade — Lester, Joe Mercer and Edward Hide — even though they were necessarily included in an earlier selection (*Flat Race Jockeys: The Great Ones*).

They ruled the roost and it is significant that Joe finished the 1979 season as Champion Jockey for the first time.

Moving up into their shoes are some excellent young riders. But one factor precludes most of them from achieving a lasting niche in the Hall of Fame. THEY *WILL* RIDE TOO SHORT!

Certainly the motor-racing champions of today are necessarily different from those of yesteryear. But racehorses and race-riding were thought of a long time before Lester Piggott. The fascinatingly varied turns and gradients of European racecourses are the same as they were in the days of Fred Archer, George Fordham, Steve Donoghue, Joe Childs and Sir Gordon Richards.

These courses and the horses who gallop on them demand horsemen — not acrobatic monkeys absurdly trying to copy the grotesque antics of our arch-acrobat, Lester Piggott.

What on earth's the matter? Are the stewards and trainers afraid of the jockeys, or are they too ignorant to know that God gave horsemen legs to drive and guide?

Don't they mind when horses lose valuable races and drop dramatically in value by swerving, being disqualified and being promptly labelled 'ungenuine'?

We know it all so well. 'A furlong out 'e was 'angin' so bad that I couldn't ride him, sir. I don't think 'e is really in love with the game.'

In fairness to owners, trainers, the general public and — above all — the horse, jockeys must be forced to let their leathers down and ride properly. For this reason I have included a photograph of one of their Australian counterparts in action today. There wasn't much wrong with Scobie Breasley, George Moore and Bill Williamson, was there?

And, if only our English jockeys *will* let their leathers down, there'll be nothing wrong with them either.

" I'LL KILL THE OLD MAN — EXPECTING ME TO WEAR SPURS!"

I

Lester Piggott

Genius — an extraordinary, natural, instinctive ability. That's what Lester has and what precious few jockeys have ever had before.

I saw it in action for the first time when I started training at Lambourn. One of the first yearlings I bought was a chestnut filly by Nasrullah, who had inherited some of her brilliant sire's temperament. The early days of a racehorse's training are vital. It is all too easy to ruin it by a stupid mistake. So, when I decided to send the newly broken youngsters upsides for the first time, I asked the then fourteen-year-old Lester to come and ride out for me.

He knew my little house in Lambourn well. It had been his school. Originally he had gone to St Alfred's in Wantage but, once he had started race-riding at the age of twelve, in order to comply with the law he used to bicycle up to have lessons with old Miss Westlake two or three times a week.

All the breaking period is fascinating, but nerve-racking – never more so than when, after they have been ridden away and taught to trot and canter in a string, you ask them to jump off and gallop two furlongs upsides for the first time. So, as Lester went down to jump the Nasrullah filly off with the others, I expected anything to happen. I needn't have worried.

While the others swerved, ducked and dived, the fourteen-year-old, sitting quite still, completely unconcerned, brought her up towards me galloping into her bridle, going as straight as a gun-barrel. It was an education which she was to appreciate for the rest of her life. She was my first winner on the flat.

You hear so much about hands, that God-given gift which combines true horsemanship with a sympathetic understanding of the animal. Few people have good hands. Lester has always had perfect hands.

The essential quality of genius is, of course, that it is born in you and Lester Keith Piggott, who was born on 5 November 1935, had all the right qualifications. His mother, Iris, was a Rickaby and sister of Bill and Fred. His father, Keith, was a magnificent, fearless jumping jockey and his grandfather, a champion jockey, rode three Grand National winners. 'I think it's harder to do that than to win the Derby three times', says his grandson, who has won the Epsom classic eight times.

By 1948, when I arrived in Lambourn as assistant trainer to Atty Persse, Keith Piggott had been training for some time at his little yard on the Eastbury Road. This was the year which saw his son, who had been riding in gymkhanas during the war years, having his first long-awaited ride in public.

He had been riding a racehorse in his father's string since he was ten, but it was not until his twelfth birthday that he was officially allowed to be apprenticed to Keith.

They lost no time. Only a fortnight after the opening of the new season Lester rode a three-year-old filly called Chase at Salisbury. But the first winner did not come until Chase had been downgraded to a Haydock seller with only 6 st 9 lbs on 18 August. Lester won by 1½ lengths. By the end of the year he had had fourteen rides, yielding a winner and two seconds.

Helped particularly by the Cundell cousins, he had 120 rides in 1949, won six races and was placed eighteen times. To the delight of the Press the thirteen-year-old beat Gordon Richards in a close finish.

Then came the crunch. Look back at those form-books and study the names of the jockeys who were riding against this brilliant, gifted boy. Most of his rivals were at least middle-aged already in 1950. There was Tommy Weston, Charlie Smirke, Charlie Elliott, Rae (Togo) Johnstone, Michael Beary, Eph and Doug Smith, Harry Carr, Ken Gethin, Billy Nevett, Cliff Richards, Tommy Lowrey, Edgar Britt, Sam and Arthur Wragg, Bill Rickaby and others of the same vintage. They were all old enough to be Lester's father. They had all made their names before the Second World War. They all expected to carry on exactly the same as before, riding for the same trainers just as though nothing had happened.

They, the local stewards and the members of the Jockey Club could not or would not understand that the ten years which included the holocaust had shattered the whole structure of British society. As has been said on more than one occasion, when a major world crisis has been greeted by record prices at the sales, racing people only seem to read the *Sporting Life* and the back pages of the other papers. They only knew that they liked their little world as they had always known it and bitterly resented any interference.

The first sign of that interference took the form of a shy, deaf, slight lad with a jumping name, poker-face, the hands of an angel and an independence worthy of Nelson. It would have been all right if he had been moderate. As it was, he was brilliant and they couldn't forgive him.

Lester explains that surly, stubborn image, which has been at the root of so much of the trouble. 'I was deaf in one ear,' he says. 'Nobody knew how I got deaf and nobody could do anything about it. But it's much better now than when I was a boy. Being a bit deaf, you did live on your own a bit. It made you a bit shy. But it had its good points. You got on with things and did them your own way, and you didn't rely on praise or blame because half the time you never heard it.'

'Not only am I not so deaf now, but I have learnt to lip-read and I watch people's faces. They're more expressive than horses' faces, but not so reliable. But even now if somebody says something when I'm not looking directly at them I may not hear. So sometimes people think I'm rude. Sometimes they think I'm disagreeing when I'm not, which is worse.'

He would arrive at the weighing room with his father, walk in, look neither to right nor to left — 'I've never been one of those "hello" people' — get changed, go out and ride his race, intent on winning. The old jockeys were unhappy, jealous and frightened.

They had always been accustomed to the old type of apprentice, who was just a little boy doing what he was told by them, the senior jockeys. In their different ways they were prepared to help a boy of this type such as they had been themselves way back in those distant pre-war days. Their help, however, was sometimes not as philanthropic as it might have been.

On the gallops Michael Beary, as stable-jockey to Atty Persse, would order the boys about, saying: 'Come up a little. Don't hang back!' or 'Pull him back to me now, you're riding work, not trying to win the gallop!' and so on.

Michael was riding in the Victoria Cup on one of the rare occasions when a Persse apprentice had a ride on a fancied horse. As the starter called them up, the lad had brought his mount into line beside the great man, only to be told by Michael in that high-pitched Irish drawl: 'This is no place for you, little boy. It's very dangerous. Get back out of it. D'you hear what I say? Get back!' Accustomed as he was to obeying Michael's orders, the boy pulled back. At that moment the tapes went up and he was hopelessly left. The danger was out of the way.

Gordon, of course, was a law unto himself. He was a colossus among midgets, ever ready to help the boys, and — however old he might pretend to be — he was, and is, younger than any of them at heart.

The remainder bitterly resented the intrusion of L. Piggott into their cosy little world, where everyone was happy in a Walter Mitty way, even though the prize-money at Royal Ascot was, in many cases, lower than it had been in the twenties.

It is fascinating (in a gruesome sort of way) to look at the list of Jockey Club members in 1944, a year before the end of hostilities and four years before the advent of Lester.

Of the forty-three members, excluding honorary members (why, incidentally, did they have to insult the Aga Khan by making him an 'honorary' member? Did they think he couldn't afford the subscription?), twelve were elected before 1916 and twenty-seven before 1930. Most of them were far too old to fight and, therefore, they survived. Thirty-one of them, excluding members of the Royal blood, had hereditary titles. Few of them had any idea how to run a sport which was developing into a vast, complex industry worth hundreds of millions of pounds in other countries.

The Duke of Portland had been elected in 1881, the Marquess of Crewe in 1895 and the Duke of Westminster in 1904. Even most of the members elected a little later were hardly more lively. More significant, apart from Lord Rosebery and Fred Withington, there was scarcely a horseman amongst them.

The blame for the decline in British racing, which had led the world since the inauguration of the sport, must be placed squarely at the door of the Jockey Club. The most important lesson I learnt as a regular officer was that I must never blame anyone under my command. 'The fish stinks from the head, sonny!' I was told. 'Nobody else is to blame but you!'

Talk about the generation gap! How could such men possibly understand the entirely new democratic thinking of the young Piggott — thinking, which, carried to extremes, has completely shattered the social structure of this country as those old men knew it. One might as well expect the MCC rulers of those days to understand and sympathize with Mick Jagger!

Look back to Newmarket in the fifties. Visit the head-quarters of racing with me as a young trainer with two runners at the meeting. Some time before, I have had to apply for car labels for my owners and for myself. Nevertheless the car park was some way from the stands.

After a three-hour drive from Lambourn and a visit to the Links Stables to inspect your horses, you queue with the other trainers and jockeys for entrance by a little turnstile alongside the weighing-room. But, even so, it is only after an argument with two rude, surly elderly gatemen that you gain admission for your wife and are reluctantly supplied with a race-card.

Check at the weighing-room that your travelling headman's declarations were in order. Then, unless you're in the first race, look for some lunch. This is provided for 'owners, provincial trainers and their wives' on long trestle tables in a sort of boiler-room, full of large pipes that feed the stand with water and heat the bottom of the back stand. It was not very good. I sympathized with the wife of one of my owners, Olivia Feilden, sister-in-law of the recent Senior Steward of the Jockey Club when she burst out one day: 'It's just like having lunch in the servants' hall!'

Of course, although we were in fact paying to provide their entertainment on their race-track, that was exactly how we were all treated by the Jockey Club — as servants. But heaven forbid that one should ever be so ill-bred and bad-mannered as to treat servants as we were sometimes treated, including important foreign visitors. It was so shaming as to make one feel embarrassed for them. I always thought they must have had very bad nannies when they were children.

Membership of Newmarket was considered very exclusive and indeed it was recognized with VIP treatment everywhere. The whole of that enormous members' stand with all its viewing, eating, drinking and other facilities was occupied only by them and, of course, by members of the Jockey Club and of the Jockey Club Rooms, who enjoyed extra privileges.

We were not allowed to cross the Members' lawn in front of their stand. If we wished to have a bet, we were forced to leave the paddock and go right round behind the stand into Tattersalls — a fair trek, particularly on a hot, crowded day.

Although the bottom tiers of the little stand looking straight down the Rowley Mile lead on to the Members' lawn, only they were allowed to use them. We ordinary trainers and jockeys were obliged to enter the stand from the back, i.e. out of the paddock, and were then confined to the pens at the top.

The first time I used this stand as a trainer I was watching a race with my wife, when we were tapped on the shoulder by another of these surly little gatemen. 'No women allowed in this side. This bit of the stand's for men only. She'll have to move over on to the women's section.' So we weren't even allowed to watch our own horses race together.

When Lester won the Linton Stakes for us on Forbear it was, of course, a great thrill to have our first success at Newmarket. But the gilt was somewhat taken off the gingerbread when we were eventually re-united with each other in the winner's enclosure. There in one corner stood some of the Jockey Club members, either staring at us disdainfully or ignoring us completely; chewing the cud and occasionally muttering to each other, like a herd of old constipated cows with bowler hats and cigars. Although some must have recognized my owners, who had been the racecourse doctors in the Midlands for many years, not one of them said 'Well done!' They never even grunted. We felt we were lucky to be allowed on this course at all and that we had in fact sinned by taking one of their prizes. It was a horrible experience on what should have been a very happy day.

Other racecourses, in varying degrees, possessed the same depressingly forbidding atmosphere of Newmarket. Looking back, it is obvious that the various degrees depended on the particular track's popularity or involvement with the Jockey Club members and their imitators among the local stewards.

So, while Ascot and Kempton were nearly as coldly controlled as Newmarket, Salisbury, Chepstow and nearly all the northern courses, influenced by racing's great impresario, Leslie Petch, remained fun.

There were no starting stalls and no camera patrol. The stewards' decisions were final and binding. There was no legal representation and no appeal against their verdicts.

By the beginning of the fifties the immediate post-war bonanza was over. Certainly churchmen were complaining about the enormous, fast-growing betting turnover, but none of it was finding its way back to the sport on which it depended. The prize-money was so abysmal that we were speedily becoming the poor relations in a world where we had been the undisputed rulers. Races at Royal Ascot were worth less than they had been in the twenties even though the cost of everything had risen astronomically.

I won four races with a fast two-year-old, Cranford Cross, including the Cuddington Stakes at Epsom, but since they totalled less than a thousand pounds the owner was actually out of pocket on the season.

The authorities didn't seem to care. In fact administration of racing was so slack that the dopers began to move in, scenting the prospect of big money with little risk of being caught and negligible penalties if they were.

This is one of the great disadvantages of the bookmaker system. So long as a criminal can make the equivalent of a bank robbery by preventing a hot favourite from winning, there will always be nobbling and attempts to bribe jockeys to stop horses.

This was the scene into which young Piggott was plunged. The Jockey Club were his masters and judges; their old, sometimes scared, favoured jockeys his rivals on the course. It could hardly have been a more disastrous introduction. In retrospect, head-on collision was inevitable.

'The jockeys were always running off to tell the stewards not just what I did, but even what I said,' he told me.

In those days you lost the right to claim an apprentice allowance after riding forty winners instead of seventy-five, now that the rule has been changed. So, well before his fourteenth birthday, Lester was riding as a fully-fledged jockey on level terms with the old ones.

Four days after his fourteenth birthday he won a race for Atty Persse on Little Bonnet at Liverpool. The old man was pleased with his handling of the little bay two-year-old filly and the following season he engaged him to ride June Ball in the Victoria Cup at Hurst Park. Unfancied at 25 to 1, Lester finished down the course.

When he came back to unsaddle, Atty, still as hard as granite despite his eighty years, came hobbling up on his two sticks with the inevitable Churchillian cigar fixed firmly between his teeth. He glared at Lester with those wide china-blue eyes. 'Well, boy?' he barked. In fifty years at the very top of his profession, he had had innumerable apprentices through his hands.

'Your filly needs a longer trip, Mr Persse,' said Lester.

Atty couldn't believe his ears. 'What did you say?'

'I said she wants further. Just because she's by a sprinter, it doesn't mean she won't stay. And she gives me the feel of a stayer.'

The blue eyes twinkled. 'How old are you, boy?'

'Fourteen, sir.'

Atty turned to Lord Sefton. 'D'you hear that, Hugh? He's all of fourteen years old and he's teaching me how to train my horses!'

Looking back now, Lester says: 'I'd still do the same. If you can't help a trainer, who can? That's what you're there for, isn't it?' He was being quite serious, by then already dedicated to his life's task of riding winners, but they laughed at first and then regarded it as gross impertinence.

Lester's own explanation of the trouble that was about to start and was to follow him through his career is typically simple. 'Old jockeys, riding for old trainers and old stewards,' he says.

In life there is always bitter resentment from moderate people who have enjoyed success against the upsurge of brilliant youth. Actors and actresses will use their experience to upstage young members of their profession, frequently with devastating effect.

By 1950, when Lester was fourteen, only Gordon Richards, then forty-six, was untouched by the success of the 'Golden Boy'. The great champion could still rely on his own immense skill to outride him. Gordon has denied that the powers that be 'had Lester in line', as they say in the Army when the authorities are determined to find fault with a soldier and bring him to book. I believe that the champion, who had always been brought up to respect authority and has always seen the best in everyone, was too good in every way to suspect that this was the case. He took things at their face value and I'm sure that, in this instance, he was wrong.

First they changed the conduct of racing in this country, where limited suspensions were virtually unknown. An offender either lost his licence, was warned off or fined. The last was a ludicrous sentence on jockeys, earning thousands of pounds a year, expecting and usually getting their presents in hard, untaxable cash. The fine, grandiosely imposed by the stewards, was merely deducted from the jockey's taxed account at Weatherby's. He never noticed it.

A certain famous jockey, riding a horse belonging to a member of the Jockey Club in a big sprint on a course where the draw was desperately important, was told: 'You've no chance from that draw.'

'Wot, me start from there in these colours?' he exclaimed.

Sure enough he started from the opposite side of the course, incurring a fine of £25. But when he duly won the race, the fine was not even a pin-prick in his thick skin.

On the other hand the 'master', in this case Lester's father, is held responsible for his apprentice's conduct. And Keith, who was no longer riding, would have felt a fine and would have taken steps to ensure that his son did not repeat the offence. Why, then, were the Piggotts not fined for alleged offences?

Lester had started 1950 still claiming the seven pounds' allowance. By the Newbury meeting on 20 October he had ridden fifty winners in that season. For minor infringements he had incurred two cautions and he had been suspended for the rest of the day at Kempton for 'injudicious riding'.

That was normal enough. It was the only form of suspension known in those days. A jockey could be suspended (though he rarely was) for the remainder of the meeting by the local stewards. Anything worse — and it had to be very bad indeed — was referred to the stewards of the Jockey Club. Then it became a sensation.

So the Newbury incident will always remain to me the most extraordinary miscarriage of justice, particularly because it led to so many more, once a precedent had been set for young Piggott. I remember it so well. Lester was riding Arthur Budgett's tough stayer, Barnacle, in the two-mile Manton Handicap. With only 7 st 7 lbs he was well in and started joint favourite at 9 to 2 with Gordon's mount, Phalorain. Third in demand at 5 to 1 was Royal Oak IV, ridden by the Australian artist, Scobie Breasley, who was — let there be no mistake — a very great jockey by any standards.

Soon after entering that long Newbury straight Lester sent Barnacle into the lead. Scobie, like all Aussies, was hugging the rails as they have to on those tight circuits of the country meetings.

Now, Keith Piggott had been a magnificent tutor for his son in every aspect of horsemanship and jockeyship except one. He had never taught him to pull his whip through or to use it in his left hand. Moreover Lester always frustrated this manoeuvre by using an extra-long whip — 'a man's whip, not a boy's whip', he said. When you remember the lightning speed with which Gordon, Steve Douglas and George Moore pulled it through and how, as young amateurs, we were made to practise for hours with reins on the foot of a bed or the back of a chair, it was very surprising still to find this chink in the armour of a great champion.

Two and a half furlongs from home, Barnacle, racing on his own now, hung over towards the rails. Scobie, veteran of a thousand such incidents, stood up in his irons and made a great show of being crossed before riding like a demon to ensure that he finished second. It was legitimate gamesmanship, which we have seen so often from that great character, Charlie Smirke.

Nevertheless, Barnacle was running on so strongly (he was to win the Great Metropolitan and the Rosebery Memorial in the following year) that Royal Oak would never have caught him in any case and Lester had no difficulty in holding off his rival's challenge to win very comfortably by three-quarters of a length. The third horse was a further four lengths away.

Scobie hurried straight into the weighing-room and lodged an objection for interference and crossing. The patrol camera, already so widely used in other countries, was, of course, unknown to British racing. So the stewards had to rely entirely on the evidence of their own eyes and of the other jockeys. As the master of the apprentice, Keith Piggott had to be called to the inquiry as well as his son. But he has never been a smooth, easy talker and there was no sympathy from these flat stewards for the former jumping star and his slim, pale, deaf boy, who shuffled in rather than marching and did not stand to attention in the approved military fashion.

They disqualified Barnacle and placed him last, a gross injustice because, although he must have won in any circumstances, he could not have been worse than second, come hell or high water. This was, however, still the normal practice in this country. The fact that the owners, who had sacrificed a valuable run and exposed their horse to the handicapper and to the betting public, were — through no fault of their own or of their trainer — hopelessly out of pocket through not receiving even the paltry second-prize money, apparently mattered not one whit.

This was bad enough. As long as I live I shall not understand what happened next. They informed Keith that the matter would be referred to the stewards of the Jockey Club. It was an amazing decision. In those early days only the most heinous of crimes were so treated. It was like sending a little boy to be tried at the Old Bailey. For, remember, in the eyes of the law Lester was just that — a very little boy of fourteen. A caution, reprimand or even perhaps suspension for the remainder of the meeting would have been adequate punishment. This was as amazing as it was inexplicably unique.

Perplexed, worried but never dreaming that strange, powerful forces were working against him, Lester rode two more winners at the meeting on horses trained by the cousins Frank and Ken Cundell. One of these was Zina, his mount in the following week's Cambridgeshire.

The Newmarket Houghton meeting opened on Tuesday. Once again the Jockey Club broke with precedent and tried Lester's case as a matter of extreme urgency. Lester and his father were marched in front of the three stewards of the Jockey Club. It was an awe-inspiring ceremony, but later Lester says: 'I wasn't afraid then and I've never been afraid since when I've been summoned before the stewards. Come to think of it, I don't think I've ever been afraid of anyone or anything.' None the less, he felt that the atmosphere was all wrong. 'Everyone seemed against me,' he said. 'It was a nasty feeling.'

They heard the evidence and they then announced their verdict. Fourteen-year-old Lester would be suspended until the end of the season, which was still more than three weeks away. In my opinion it was a savage sentence, which branded him for the future. That was how it all started. The Establishment had shown what they thought of the most brilliant young jockey to come under their jurisdiction. No encouragement or guidance from the top — just hammer down with a feudal blunt instrument. All Jockey Club members, it has been said, are old by the time they are twenty-three. This particular vintage had, it appeared, decided that the Piggotts must be put, and kept, firmly in their place.

As the headlines screamed '£10,000-a-year boy suspended', Lester had the consolation of knowing that the last laugh would surely be his. Out of 403 rides that season he had scored fifty-two wins, forty-five seconds and thirty-nine thirds. When the curtain fell at Manchester on 18 November, he was eleventh on the jockeys' list, just one behind Charlie Elliott, in front of men like Joe Sime, Ken Gethin and Charlie Smirke.

Now there appeared the first of those temperamental horses with which Lester has been associated and which have proved conclusively to me that he is one of the greatest 'naturals' of all time. Remember how he performed on my Nasrullah yearling? Zucchero was by Nasrullah, too, out of a mare by Bois Roussel — a combination which had imparted brilliance and stamina, but also a fair bit of temperament. As a two-year-old he won a race and gave an indication of his vast potential by finishing second in the New Stakes at Royal Ascot. Then he developed a dislike for the starting gate just as another Nasrullah colt, his speedy contemporary, Grey Sovereign, had done. At the end of that season he was transferred by his owner, George Rolls, from Michael Blackmore at Whatcombe to Ken Cundell, who was already helping young Piggott on his way. The big brown colt and the fifteen-year-old boy met for the first time on the Compton gallops and struck up an instant friendship.

After finishing fourth in the seven-furlong Henry VIII Stakes at Hurst Park, the new partnership moved on to Epsom for the Blue Riband Trial Stakes, run over the last mile and 110 yards of the Derby course.

On the big day, however, it was not to be. The preliminaries proved too much for Zucchero. It was, however, a valuable experience for the lad, who was later to make that tricky Epsom track and the world's greatest race his own.

There is a photograph in Lester's cuttings book of the

Derby field galloping off into the distance leaving Zucchero far behind at the starting gate. Here is actual evidence, rivalled only by that remarkable picture of The Tetrarch at the start of Sandown's five-furlong National Breeders' Produce Stakes. 'The Spotted Wonder' is on his knees with the tapes caught in his teeth, as the rest of the field jumps off. At a conservative estimate he was left twenty lengths. You will never realize how stiff that Sandown five miles is unless you go down and stand at the start. Only here on this sensational horse could Steve Donoghue have achieved the impossible. He sat still and waited until the field came back to him and got in the last strides to win by a short head.

Although Zucchero did not win the Derby, he put up a remarkable performance once Lester finally persuaded him to start running through the field to finish thirteenth of thirty, three behind Arctic Prince.

'I have no doubt at all,' says his jockey, 'that, if Zucchero had got off with the others, he must have won.'

Zucchero won his next three races, including the Commonwealth Stakes at Sandown, where he beat the St James's Palace winner, Turco II, by six lengths. 'He was always left, but we sort of understood each other,' says Lester. 'I still say he was one of the best horses I've ever ridden.'

The King George VI and Queen Elizabeth Festival of Britain Stakes at Ascot on 21 July had attracted a worthy international field: the two Guineas winners, Ki Ming and Belle of All; the Derby winner, Arctic Prince; François Mathet's superb actioned Tantième, who had just taken the Coronation Cup; the previous year's Leger winner, Marcel Boussac's Scratch II; Sir Winston Churchill's Colonist; Mossborough, Wilwyn, Supreme Court and four more Frenchmen. There were nineteen runners in all.

Once again Zucchero was slowly away and Lester found himself at the back of the field with Supreme Court, ridden by that great international rider, Charlie Elliott. Manny Mercer set a strong gallop on Wilwyn, so that he and most of his rivals were nearly done with as they entered the straight. Here Jacko Doyasbère lost his chance by going too wide on Tantième.

A furlong out Supreme Court took it up, but Lester still had a bit in hand. The two English colts battled it out and at the finish Elliott just held on to win by three-quarters of a length. The third, Tantième, was six lengths away.

On this showing Zucchero looked a good thing for the St Leger. It would have been sensational if Lester could have won a classic at the age of fifteen. However, three weeks before the Doncaster race he broke his leg in a heavy fall at Lingfield and was out for the rest of the season.

Zucchero obviously resented his substitute jockey, Charlie Spares, sulked and finished ninth of eighteen in the Leger behind the Boussac colt Talma II, who, ridden by Rae Johnstone, spreadeagled his field in the most extraordinary way.

Although he was grounded on 25 August with nearly three months of the season to go, Lester had already had 432 rides compared with 403 the previous year. They had produced fifty-one winners, including the Eclipse on that charming French colt Mystery IX.

Lester still reckons that he should have won the Derby in the following year, 1952. As it was, he came in for a certain amount of ridicule, which was totally unjustified and was mostly inspired by such quips as 'What did I Tulyar?' and so on.

Scobie Breasley, Neville Sellwood and Billy Cook had returned to Australia. So in Scobie's fortunately temporary absence, Lester rode for Druids Lodge and had the mount on Gay Time in the Derby.

Tulyar was a very good little horse, with that thrilling action possessed by the best. When they are fully extended, they seem to drop about a foot — actually 'getting down to it' and almost justifying the description *ventre à terre*. But the Aga Khan's colt, whose one two-year-old success had been in the Buggins Farm Nursery at Haydock, was, in Lester's opinion, still short of his best when the Derby came.

Gay Time was the sort of horse that I personally dislike — a large, light chestnut with a flaxen mane and tail, generally signs of softness. He was a grandson by Rockafella of Hyperion and had a distinct look of the great little stallion's son, the Queen's Aureole, who was then a two-year-old. Both these two were the exception to the rule. Although highly strung, they were very game.

Unhappily, everything conspired against Gay Time at Epsom. He pulled a plate off in the paddock before the race and, after having been replated, had to go down to the start

by himself. This was no picnic for a highly strung thoroughbred in the fairground atmosphere of Epsom Downs on
Derby Day. By the time he had made his way through the
shouting, down that pathway past the blaring noise of the
swings and roundabouts and up the other side to another
mass of people thronging the starting gate, he was in a muck
lather. He had virtually lost his race already.

Nevertheless he was made of sterner stuff than his appearance indicated. A slow beginner, he was unable to lay up in
the early stages. He was drawn on the outside of a large field
of thirty-three runners. As always, those with little chance
determined to make a show, galloping as fast as they could
up that long pull to the top of Tattenham Hill. When, equally
inevitably, they began to fall back beaten, Lester was forced
to come wide, thereby losing a lot of valuable ground.

Rounding Tattenham Corner into the straight, Smirke sent
Tulyar into the lead, but now Gay Time slipped into top gear
and, galloping on resolutely, began to make up ground and
overhaul the little boy. How close he would have got is anyone's guess. Lester is convinced he would have won if Tulyar
had not come across him below the distance and checked him
before going on to win by three lengths. Lester determined to
object. Knowing the attitude of the hierarchy to their young
star, it was most unlikely that his complaint would have been
entertained and the Aga Khan's colt disqualified. In the event
how happy they must have been.

The boy jockey was tired. Gay Time, a big heavy colt was
tired and sprawling. The pull-up at Epsom was the worst in
the world, except for a point-to-point course I remember
near Taunton, where we had to pull up into a brick wall!

Lester says: 'As I tried to pull him up, Gay Time collided
with the rails, fell over on his head, throwing me off, and
then galloped away into the wood behind the paddock. When
he was eventually found, and I arrived back at the weighing-
in room to weigh in, lots of people said I had grounds for
objection. So I told the Clerk of the Scales that I wanted to
lodge an official objection to the winner for crossing and
taking my ground.'

The Clerk of the Scales looked at him and said bluntly,
'You're too late to object!'

This was the Derby. Even in 1952 the difference to the
owner of a potential stallion between winning and losing was

several hundred thousand pounds. Even if he was late (which Lester still disputes) it was due to an unavoidable, painful accident.

The relevant rule of racing has been slightly altered. In the 1952 Rule Book, Rule 168 (iv) read: 'An objection to a horse on the ground of a cross, jostle or any act on the part of the jockey . . . must be made within five minutes after the winner has been weighed in, unless, under special circumstances, the Stewards are satisfied that it could not have been made within that time.'

How could they have possibly signalled 'All right', when the runner-up in the world's most important race was still missing? Were these not special circumstances?

This was the year when John Schapiro, who, with his father, had taken over the Laurel Park race-track in Maryland, made history by inaugurating the Washington International. The first two English horses to accept invitations were Wilwyn and his easy Ascot conqueror, Zucchero. Manny Mercer, the other young hopeful of British racing, was to ride Wilwyn. Lester, who, as we have seen, really understood the horse, was to have been on Zucchero.

Unfortunately, George Rolls chose this moment to change trainers again and sent the colt from Ken Cundell, who had a claim on Lester's services, to Bill Payne, another friend of the Piggotts, who very much wanted to maintain the successful horse-jockey relationship. Ken and his owners would not let Lester go. They needed him in England. The seeds of that famous freelance decision were undoubtedly planted at a tender age. Charlie Smirke was substituted.

Now Lester, who knew the horse so well, had always accepted the fact that Zucchero would be slowly away from the start. Smirke determined to get him away on terms at all costs. He was a great horseman and he succeeded. But the tactics were mistaken. The colt, surprised, took a tremendous hold and fought for his head all the way, so that he had nearly had enough when he took the lead entering that short straight. He was run out of it by Wilwyn and the American entry, Rube.

'He would have won easily if I had ridden him', says Lester. 'He was a different class.'

This is indisputable. He had proved it at Ascot. But in fairness to Charlie, the sharp American circuit may have been at least partly responsible for the hard pulling. Horses are apt to dislike our wide staring English course, whereas they love going round bends. This is always the time when they will try to run away and will do so if you let them. Bald Eagle, who won two Washington Internationals, and Amerigo were perfect examples of this. They resented English tracks but came into their own in the United States.

Now twenty-eight years have brought us to the 1980s. John Schapiro's dream has almost come true. When Lester and the English Derby winner, Sir Ivor, won the International, it was indeed a great moment. Unfortunately the risk of infection produced a ban on the importation of horses to Europe from America in 1971, which set the race back badly. John's tremendous enthusiasm and hard work deserved to succeed. As one who helped him in recent years, I can vouch for the innumerable difficulties he had had to overcome. We will return to Washington later for Lester's triumphs and his row with the American Press.

In 1953 the Piggott Derby winner was Prince Charlemagne, a handsome colt, who was not up to classic standard but whom Lester rode to victory in the Triumph Hurdle during the spring of the next momentous year in his career.

Old Joe Lawson, now training at Newmarket, had a backward American three-year-old for Robert Sterling Clark, called Never Say Die, a big liver-chestnut son of Nasrullah. Ridden by Scobie Breasley, now happily returned from Australia, he had finished third in his last race of the season, the Dewhurst Stakes.

Lester rode Never Say Die in his first race as a three-year-old, the Union Jack Stakes at Liverpool. They finished second. Then Manny Mercer had the mount in the Newmarket Stakes and was third behind Elopement, the chestnut full-brother to Gay Time.

Suddenly out of the blue a telegram arrived at the Piggotts' Lambourn home from Joe Lawson. It said simply: 'You ride Never Say Die in Derby.' One of the oldest trainers had selected the youngest jockey.

He had no cause to regret his choice. Eighteen-year-old Lester handled the colt with all the superb cool of a veteran to win comfortably by two lengths from Arabian Night with Manny Mercer on Darius a neck away third.

If Joe Lawson had been younger, I don't think he would

have run his Derby winner again at Royal Ascot. He would have realized that the colt was so one-sided that he acted badly on a right-handed track. This, too, was probably due to the trainer's age and lack of his supervision when the colt was broken.

From birth everything conspires to make a horse left-handed. As soon as he has his little headcollar on, he is led on the nearside. So when you start to lunge him, he automatically goes round to his left. And, unless he has been particularly well handled at stud, he will resent being sent round to the right when the trainer starts to break him as a yearling. If you don't persevere at this stage, someone is in for a lot of trouble later on. This is one of the advantages of driving on long reins. You can make the animal go just as easily to the right as to the left.

In the past the Irish have been great sinners in this respect. Many an expensive potential jumper has had to be remade before he can achieve the even balance required in a top-class performer. I remember Fulke Walwyn and Bryan Marshall having awful trouble with Dorothy Paget's splendid young jumpers when they first arrived from Ireland. Inevitably, it seemed, they were all left-handed.

So was Never Say Die to a marked degree. It did not matter in the Derby because the Epsom track is left-handed and Lester gave the horse a smooth, easy ride to win comfortably.

Ascot, on the other hand, is constantly turning to the right, and Lester knew that he would have his work cut out to keep his horse balanced in the King Edward VII Stakes, in which he was giving eight pounds to the Epsom runner-up. So, at the weights, Arabian Night was just favourite at 13 to 8 with the Derby winner at 7 to 4. Rashleigh, trained by Noel Murless and ridden by Sir Gordon Richards in his last season, was third in demand at 5 to 1. Gordon had just returned to the saddle after being laid off with injury following that nasty crash at Salisbury.

In fairness, I will give both jockeys' accounts of the controversial Ascot race, which sparked off one of the racing sensations of the decade:

Gordon: 'Coming into the straight, Blue Prince and Dragon Fly were making the running, with Rickaby on Garter third, Gosling on Arabian Night fourth, and I was fifth. Dragon Fly dropped out, and Rickaby and I began to move up to the leader. All of a sudden, Lester Piggott on Never Say Die started to make a move. I was on the outside, and so I do not know whether Never Say Die was hanging or not. Lester claimed he was. At any rate, Never Say Die charged into Garter, and Garter hit my quarters and practically turned me round. Then Never Say Die charged Garter again, and Garter turned me broadside on. I suspect that it did look, from the Stand, as if my horse was doing the damage; but if another horse hits yours in the rump, it will throw you into him, and that is what happened.

'Rashleigh recovered marvellously, and he and Tarjoman — being ridden by that splendid French jockey, Poincelet — went on to challenge Arabian Night who had taken up the running with Blue Prince. Arabian Night dived twice, first of all putting Blue Prince on to Tarjoman, and then Tarjoman on to me. But Rashleigh would not be beaten whatever happened to him, and he went on to win.

'Of course it was a most unsatisfactory race, and the stewards objected to me. But immediately they had heard the evidence, they withdrew their objection.

'They did, however, stand Lester Piggott down.'

Lester: 'It all happened soon after we entered the straight. I was lying handy on the rails. As there were three horses in front of me, who were beginning to weaken, I decided to switch to the outside to give my horse a chance of a long, unimpeded run with that great stride of his.

'As I started to move, however, one of the leaders dropped back and, at that moment Gordon came from behind further outside and proceeded to ride in. First he lay on the other horse. Then, although looking across, he could see I hadn't much room, he pushed the other horse (I think it was Lord Rosebery's Garter, ridden by Bill Rickaby) right on top of me. Of course there was a big bump and the other horse was half turned. My horse was hanging too, towards his favourite left-hand side, which, of course, didn't help matters. Anyway Gordon went on and won by a length. I finished fourth.

'As soon as we got back, the stewards objected to Gordon — rightly, in my opinion — but when they heard the evidence of the other jockeys they withdrew the objection and turned their attention to me, claiming that I had been trying to force my way out.'

Clive Graham of the *Daily Express* said: 'Piggott and Never Say Die began to move half a mile out when he saw an opening between Dragon Fly (Doug Smith) and Garter (Bill Rickaby). When he was half-way there, the horses came together and there was a collision.'

I saw the race and I'm not going to take sides. I think that a certain amount of blame for the incident could be attached to Gordon, Lester and Tommy Gosling. Certainly it was by no means an open-and-shut case.

But once again, the Ascot stewards, with no film to guide them, completely exonerated everyone but Lester. They listened to the evidence of the other jockeys and heard his stumbling version. Then they suspended him for the remainder of the meeting and reported him to the stewards of the Jockey Club.

The Duke of Norfolk headed the Cavendish Square inquiry. This seemed strange to me at the time because of his connection with Ascot. Once again there was no question of a caution or a fine, even though the issue was so controversial. They suspended Lester for six months and ordered his father to send him to another trainer.

Lester says: 'I was absolutely dumbfounded. I just couldn't believe it. Again I felt that everyone was against me and I still insist that this was an unnecessary, savage sentence, which did no good at all.'

He was ordered to leave home and go to Newmarket to 'do his two' and ride out under the instruction of Lord Rosebery's trainer, Jack Jarvis. 'As the old man was sick in bed the whole time I was there,' says Lester, 'that was a fat lot of good!'

Few people realized what suspension meant to the dedicated boy. 'My life stopped,' he says, 'because racing is my whole life. It's my work and my pleasure at one and the same time. Apart from my family it provides me with all the fun I ever need. Which, of course, is why I never want a holiday.'

The blow was struck at the height of the season. Apart from all the other winners, he missed riding Never Say Die in the Leger. Charlie Smirke substituted for him and won by twelve lengths.

That race alone was worth £13,372. Clark was a very generous owner and would have given his winning rider more than ten per cent of the stake. So, purely from a financial point of view, the sentence must have cost the Piggotts thousands of pounds.

The same *'Racing Calendar'* that carried the official announcement of Lester's six-month sentence reported that Manny Mercer had been fined £50 for striking Davy Jones with his whip in a race.

How can you possibly reconcile the two sentences? It is hard to escape the thought that poor little Manny, one of the nicest and best jockeys ever to grace the turf, was retained by a number of Jockey Club members.

After Doncaster perhaps the Jockey Club realized that they had overstepped the mark. They lifted the ban a fortnight after the Leger, when Lester had served just over three months of his sentence. On 4 October he was appointed to succeed Gordon as first jockey to Noel Murless, who handled many horses for Jockey Club members. Lester could be pardoned for thinking that it was a strange world.

It was a highly successful, but always uneasy, partnership. There was that day at Ascot when Lester had ridden a placed horse for the Queen, who was a little slow arriving in the unsaddling enclosure from the royal box. Her jockey, who was riding in the next, touched his black velvet cap, muttered 'Thank you, Ma'am,' and hurried off into the weighing-room.

Noel came storming after him, 'The Queen wanted to talk to you,' he fumed.

'Oh, what did she want?' asked Lester, raising that blank, innocent face.

'She wanted to say that she doesn't like ill-mannered little b——s riding for her!'

Still, Noel headed the trainers' list four times with Lester. They won two Derbys with Crepello and St Paddy, and Lester won the jockeys' championship in 1960, '64, '65 and '66 — the season when the sensational break-up occurred.

It was in 1962, when he was due to ride Noel's Young Lochinvar in the Derby, that Lester had his next big brush with the authorities, who so often seem to have people up for the wrong offences.

It happened at an evening meeting at Lincoln on 30 May, a week before the Derby. Bob Ward was a likeable selling-plate specialist who had been training for sixteen years at Hednesford in Staffordshire. He was not the Establishment's favourite trainer.

Bob had two runners in the same race: Polly Macaw and Ione. Lester was booked for the latter, who opened at odds-on for this very reason. Soon, however, she dropped in the betting as money came in for her stable-companion, who was justifiably installed as favourite in her stead.

'As soon as we jumped off I realized that the punters were right. My filly had no possible hope of beating Polly Macaw. So, rather than give the little thing a hiding, I did my best until I found that she had nothing more to give and then I dropped my hands.'

Major-General Sir Randle Feilden, who had not yet risen to his eminent state as Chairman of the Turf Board, thought it was a bad case, accused Ward and Piggott of stopping Ione and referred the matter to the stewards of the Jockey Club.

'I told them the truth,' says Lester, 'that Ione could never and would never beat Polly Macaw and that she was utterly useless, as she later proved. But they obviously didn't believe me.'

He was suspended until the end of July and Bob's licence was taken away indefinitely. On this occasion Lester was very angry. Faced with the prospect of two months of nail-biting frustration and the loss of an immense sum of money, he had a right to go at the reporters, who beseiged his house when he returned home to Newmarket. He hit one hard on the jaw and then chased them off, throwing stones out of his garden at them.

Lester had married Susan Armstrong on 22 February 1960. He celebrated by being champion jockey for the first time.

When, on his twenty-fifth birthday, Lester found himself champion jockey, I talked to Sir Gordon, his predecessor at Warren Place. It was a most revealing interview with the great champion, who had doubted whether Lester would top the list because of his weight.

'If only he were seven pounds lighter,' said the man who had filled that position for the first time ten years before Lester was born.

We talked about the will-power and determination of this young man, who, built on the tall mould of Fred Archer, had had to overcome more obstacles to success than any other rider since Archer, beaten in his battle against weight, killed himself in 1886.

Though he had had to see his own jockey, Scobie Breasley, take second place in the riders' table, Gordon was as delighted with Piggott's success as if he had won the championship again himself.

'By resisting the temptation to eat and by depriving himself of all the good things of life that a young man wants, Lester has shown the most amazing strength of character,' he said.

'The secret of his success is confidence. Confidence in his own genius. For he is a genius as Steve Donoghue was before. From the very beginning he has always known instinctively exactly what to do and when to do it.

'Take Epsom, the trickiest course of them all. Lester never worries about the bends or the crowding or what all the other jockeys are doing. Like Steve, he gets into exactly the right position — about fourth or fifth — and then at the psychological moment he goes. That was how he won the 1957 Oaks on Carrozza. This was one of the best races he has ever ridden.

'Just think of it! He was only twenty-one . . . riding for the Queen . . . and it was the Oaks. But it made no difference to Lester. He behaved just as if it had been a selling race and at precisely the right moment, before the other jockeys knew what was happening, he went. Believe me, he stole that race.'

Then I asked Gordon about the cheekiness and rough riding, which had threatened to ruin the young champion's career. He answered firmly: 'A lot of nonsense has been talked and written about Lester's behaviour on and off a horse.

'For example, that story about him calling me Grandpa was quite untrue. Of course he would stand up for himself if necessary, but I always found him respectful and well-mannered.

'None of the rough riding was deliberate. It was all part and parcel of his genius. He just knew that he had to be in a certain place at a certain time to win.'

I shall quote Gordon on Lester again. But this was the most important verdict from the champion of champions at a time when he had been out of the saddle for only six years.

When Lester had stopped growing, he started to pull his stirrup leathers up. I have a photograph of him winning the Linton Stakes at Newmarket for me on Forbear in 1954 and he is riding at a normal length. He could use those splendid long legs for the purpose for which they were designed – to drive and guide.

Many of our recent top jockeys – Geoff Lewis, George Moore, Jimmy Lindley, Bill Williamson – rode at about the classic length like Steve Donoghue, Michael Beary and Charlie Elliott. Gordon used to ride almost the full length of his little legs.

I have aroused the wrath of certain fellow-journalists through criticizing Lester's ultra-short leathers. How dare I find fault with the master? Well, as a professional horseman, I stick to my guns. I think that's what journalism is all about. You are paid to be a critic, not a sychophant and, if you are convinced that you are right, you should always say so. Anyway, Lester only laughs about it when I tell him he just does it out of bloody-mindedness, pulling his leathers up so short that he is almost standing on the saddle.

'I've been pulling them up all the time,' he says, 'and I'm still pulling them up! Although I may not look very comfortable, I feel more comfortable. Everybody has to ride the way he feels most comfortable.'

He goes on: 'One of the disadvantages of being tall is style. Style is the way you look. If you're small, it doesn't matter so much how you look, because there isn't so much of you to be seen and your legs don't take up so much room. If you're big you can be seen better and there's less horse showing. I smile when people ask why I ride with my bottom in the air. I've got to put it somewhere, haven't I? Anyway it works and I'm comfortable.'

This is undeniable. But I have seen him lose races he ought to have won. When a horse starts hanging badly he has no legs to correct him and so he must use his whip. But, as we have seen, he still lacks dexterity in pulling his weapon through and in using it with his left hand.

Furthermore, I think he is always at the risk of losing a race on an objection. Although horses go uncannily straight for him, there is always the odd one that swerves under pressure, which could mean the sacrifice of a major prize. Lastly, great horseman that he is, he is more likely to be unseated than if he had been riding with longer leathers, as we have seen on several occasions like the day when Ribero dropped him and galloped off to eat rhododendrons before the King George VI and Queen Elizabeth Stakes at Ascot.

'Horses have always run straight for me,' he says. 'Ever since I first started riding work as a kid. I suppose I'm especially lucky. To me it's just instinct. I'm so used to a horse going straight that, if he gets on the wrong leg, I can just put him right. I don't even think about it.'

So while still insisting that this beautifully natural horseman would be better advised to ride longer than he does I freely admit that his unorthodox style has been wonderfully successful — for him.

This is one of the major troubles. Other jockeys and, in particular, apprentices, inevitably imitate the champion. See how Stan Mellor modelled himself on Fred Winter, while Geoff Lewis deliberately copied Gordon.

Lester's father-in-law, Sam Armstrong, said: 'It's becoming increasingly difficult as stable lads and apprentices, copying Lester, pull their knees up to their chins. He can ride like that, but they can't. It's bad for them and for the horses, whose mouths are bound to suffer.'

Sam, one of our finest horsemasters, went on: 'The style seems to suit Lester. Horses appear to run for him with his weight just forward of the point of balance. But it doesn't work for anyone else.'

Arthur Budgett, breeder-owner-trainer of two Derby winners, agreed wholeheartedly. 'All the boys try to copy Lester,' said the former Whatcombe trainer. 'I was always having to make them let their leathers down. It's disastrous. They're so insecure that, if they don't fall off, they're hanging on to the horse's mouth.'

Even as Lester passed the Epsom winning post on St Paddy in the 1960 Derby, the favourite, Angers, was shot by the course vet, James Garrett, who had been following the field in the official car. The French were furious. They believed that the Strassburger colt, for whom bookmaker William Hill had offered £200,000 a week earlier, could have been saved for stud.

But Garrett, finding the colt on three legs two furlongs down Tattenham Hill, like that other French favourite, Holocaust, in 1899, had no hesitation.

'There was nothing else I could do,' said the vet. 'The horse's near foreleg was smashed to smithereens. The fetlock and cannon-bone were broken and the horse had a split pastern.'

He was probably right. So much depends on the horse's

individual constitution and temperament and Angers was a highly-strung colt. You need a very sensible sort of thorough-bred to endure months in plaster as well as all the intricate surgery required.

However, Ryan Price and his vet did achieve success around this time with a far humbler French colt called York, who recovered from multiple fractures to win two hurdle races and was subsequently given to me. And Europe's top vet, Dr Edouard Pouret, had a remarkable and much publicized similar success when a very valuable potential stallion smashed his leg at Longchamp in 1971.

One thing is certain. If an animal's genital organs are undamaged, it is crazy not to make an effort to save a well-bred colt or filly for stud. For years, frightened of charges of cruelty, our racecourse vets have been somewhat trigger-happy. One of the major faults of English horsemastership, horsemanagement and, indeed, horsemanship, is that too many people in this country credit animals with the same feelings and minds as human beings.

In fact, since a horse has no imagination and a very small brain, it does not suffer pain to the same extent as a human. Watch a horse being fired or castrated by a good vet and you will know what I mean. So I believe that public opinion should be re-educated to recognize the humanity in curing an animal, which can subsequently enjoy a happy, productive life at stud, rather than 'putting it out of its misery'. It is terrifying how a bullet can convert half a million pounds to fifty pounds in a split second.

But, of course, this is the other side of the coin. Insurance companies only pay out on death. They give nothing, despite their large premiums, to compensate owners of horses that can never race again but which will cost a fortune in keep and vet's bills while attempts are being made to save them. Many owners would prefer to recoup their outlay from the insurance with that quick, humane, racecourse vet's bullet than risk the alternative.

The following day at Epsom, Lester broke another record. He became the fastest man on four legs in the world.

The world speed record by a horse had been set up way back in 1933 — two years before our hero was born. A three-year-old filly called Devineress, carrying 7 st 5 lbs, clocked 54.6 secs for the sharp Epsom five furlongs.

In the Tadworth Handicap Stakes with the big weight of 9 st 5 lbs, but with the invaluable aid of Lester, four-year-old Indigenous smashed the record by one whole second, recording an incredible 53.6 secs.

The rulers of the turf in 1960 took little trouble, it seemed, to present good, entertaining sport to the public. Nobody bothered about watering the racecourses, for example. One day during that summer, Nottingham provided one of the most ludicrously bad afternoons' racing in the history of the sport. Eighteen runners had turned out for six races. There were *two* walkovers, two fields of three, and two of five. Although there was (and is) a certain amount of validity in the executive's excuse that there was too much racing at this time of year, the main reason for such low numbers of runners unquestionably was the unnecessarily hard going.

Always we seemed to be given the same answer. 'It's nothing to do with us. It's up to the courses concerned.'

The Jockey Club and local stewards were still keeping the public in the dark in 1960. Inquiries were held in private and objections were either sustained or overruled with no explanation to the punters who lost their money.

By then doping was rife. Doping to stop. The kind of doping which is so profitable in a country where bookmakers still hold sway. Under a Tote monopoly, such as is enjoyed throughout the rest of the civilized world, you can't lay against a hot favourite, knowing that it is 'dead meat'. You can here. What's more you can make many thousands of pounds with very little risk of detection. And, if you are caught, you'll probably get no more than a year for conspiracy to defraud.

A famous American millionaire said at the time: 'Nothing would induce me to leave a horse in training in England. We put our own house in order some years ago when we abolished bookmakers and I do not want to get involved in a dirty sport again. Your racing stinks!'

Still retained in 1960 was that outrageous rule of racing, which was habitually feared by every trainer — Rule 176(II) — which read: 'If in any case, in which the stewards have ordered a horse to be examined it shall be found that any drug or stimulant has been administered to a horse for the purpose of affecting its speed in a race, the licence of the trainer shall be withdrawn and he shall be declared a dis-qualified person.'

I shall never understand how such a grotesquely unfair rule could have been countenanced. A casual word misinterpreted could have caused a test to be taken, and a trainer's entire livelihood could easily depend on the whim of another person.

But the rule was kept and acted on until the Arundel horses, Red Letter and Skymaster, were found to have been doped. It was not, of course, a Jockey Club inquiry. The Duke of Norfolk revealed the dope findings but his trainer was not tried under Rule 176(II).

More controversy was to follow. On 15 August I wrote for the *Daily Mail* from Newbury: 'Newbury's stewards, led by former Rhine Army commander General Sir Miles Dempsey, on Saturday missed a heaven-sent opportunity of restoring public faith in the impartial rules of the Jockey Club and of retrieving the badly damaged, tumbling prestige of British racing. They should have ordered an official examination of Kipling.

'Consider the facts. In the 1 mile 600 yd Oxfordshire Stakes, watched by thousands of punters on the course and on TV, the evens-money favourite, Lord Sefton's St Leger colt, Kipling, who had won his last three races and beaten St Paddy, the Derby winner, at Goodwood, finished tailed off last. He was more than twenty lengths behind the winner, High Hat, and fifteen lengths behind his own pacemaker, Tobago (second).

'Jockey Geoff Lewis agreed that Kipling ran a long way below form. Said Geoff: 'It was no gallop. Kipling's poor showing was due to nothing that I can account for.'

'Trainer Peter Hastings-Bass said he was not satisfied with the colt's running.

'But, although Peter, acting on the friendly advice of a vet, had a saliva test taken at his Kingsclere stables, no official test was taken on the course.

'If the stewards had ordered such a test, and, if Mrs Munday, the Jockey Club analyst, had returned a positive result, Peter's training licence would have had to be with-drawn and Kipling would have been barred from racing again.

'On the other hand, such a test would have exposed once and for all the injustice of the present rule, for the outstanding integrity of owner and trainer in this case is well known.

'Even if it were not, it is obvious that Kipling's connections could only lose by defeat of their favourite.

'Peter does not bet, and Lord Sefton, an owner-breeder, stood to lose thousands of pounds in the depreciated value of a potential stallion.

'Thus, as in the recent case of the Duke of Norfolk's Skymaster, another potential stallion, only a criminal book-maker, or someone else in a position to lay the favourite, could benefit from Kipling's defeat and from the subsequent loss of punters' money.

'An official test on Kipling might well have proved negative but, in the interests of Lord Sefton, of Peter Hastings-Bass, of the little owners and trainers, and of British sport itself, it should have been taken — if only to prove that in racing, there is not one law for the rich and one for the poor.'

Eleven days later I reported again:

'With the new jumping season already under way in the West Country, a terrifying fresh slant on this doping business was put to me at Brighton by Ryan Price, king of National Hunt trainers and employer of Fred Winter, greatest jumping jockey of our time.

'Said Ryan: "This nobbling of favourites is bad enough on the flat. But unless it is stopped before jumping starts in earnest jockeys could easily be killed. Just think if anything should happen to Fred?"

'Ryan is right. If the police fail to find the culprits before November when the flat ends and N.H. racing becomes the medium of the nation's gambling, manslaughter could well be done.

'For the drug which merely makes a favourite drowsy and incapable of exerting himself fully has no disastrous con-sequences on the flat.

'But imagine if you can, the shattering fall when a dopey horse tries to negotiate an obstacle at speed.'

And again, on 27 August, when it was becoming obvious that in order to get at horses the dopers must be employing lads or ex-lads, who were so hopelessly underpaid, despite a five-year apprenticeship, that they would be desperate to earn some easy money:

'August, normally the dullest month, this year finds British racing simmering with frustration and discontent.

'Among the post-war industries, racing is unique in that it is the only one not to recognize the old service axiom that the interests of the worker — the chap who actually tends the production line — must be studied before those of anyone else.

'For example, despite the pathetic little stable lads' strike, when the Betting Bill was in committee stage early this year, nobody — as far as we have been told — produced the one argument likely to influence modern politicians and top business-men: that is, that the only reasons for owners needing more prize money is to enable them to pay more to their trainers and lads.

'After all, no one is compelled to own a racehorse any more than he is forced to buy a Rolls-Royce.

'It is important to remember that, despite remuneration which makes our sport the laughing stock of the world, the English form book works out to a remarkable degree. Thus the integrity of our working trainers and lads is still the envy of all — yet these men are never consulted on any of the major matters of policy which affect their lives and their livelihoods.

'Furthermore, neither they nor the public are kept 'in the picture' about the operational, disciplinary or administrative side of racing — with the result that, instead of narrowing in keeping with the times, the gulf between rulers and ruled widens terrifyingly.

'As the trainer shamefacedly pays out all that he can afford — about £9 each a week — to lads working a seven-day week, he hears that the average wage for dockers, asking for more money and a forty-one hour week, is already £15.

'What is the Jockey Club going to do about it? No information or friendly guidance is given.

'It may not be generally known that the ruling body, through their secretaries, forces a trainer to pay a jockey's retainer (which has to be recovered from the owners) but refuses to help the trainer in any way to recover money owed to him by defaulting owners. Fines are imposed with monotonous regularity, but no one knows where the money goes.

'It is proposed to popularize racing at Newmarket — surely a big-business venture requiring the know-how of a Jack Hylton — but a committee of well-meaning amateurs is formed to deal with an issue which affects the livings of all the professionals. At least, that is what we are told — and with no further information, we can only assume the worst.

'So the feeling of grievance and sense of injustice among the professionals, about, for instance, the application of the dope policy (if indeed one exists), is very real.

'I have gone into this in some detail because the popular Press is being called sensation-seeking and irresponsible, whereas it is, in fact, speaking very responsibly for the men who are the backbone of racing.

'Only repeated official explanations and assurances can dispel this horrible feeling of uneasiness and distrust, which haunts our racecourses.'

It was a horrible season in 1960 for all but Lester, who won the Leger so easily on St Paddy and finished up as the new champion jockey. Even he was to suffer from the dopers the following year.

During the winter we managed a few steps forward. The Duke of Norfolk led a three-man dope investigation and the Jockey Club finally surrendered to tremendous pressure and introduced overnight declarations from the start of the new flat season.

Immediately I demanded the common-sense reform of overnight blinkers. But I was constantly told this would be 'interfering with the rights of owners' and we had to wait another eleven years before they were introduced. We are still waiting for overnight jockeys.

While on the subject of reforms, it is worth noting that on New Year's Day 1961, Ryan Price came out strongly in favour of women riders, who had just been introduced in France. He was on his own.

What an uncivilized world it was. Not only was Vincent O'Brien wrongly accused and convicted but also he was not even allowed to live in his own home, lovely Ballydoyle, until the end of a season in which his horses took his stand-in brother, Phonsie, to the top of the trainers' list. His owner, Frank Burmann, was leading owner. The horse which put them there was none other than the alleged dope victim, Chamour, who later won the Irish Derby.

Second in the owners' table was the Turf Club Senior Steward, Joe McGrath, who presided over the inquiry which resulted in Vincent's suspension. It could only happen in Ireland. It looked as though they would have to call on the 'little people' to sort out the comic-opera situation, which the Irish Stewards had created for themselves.

In the end, Vincent started training again in May 1961, twelve months after his suspension. He was completely vindicated in court and, graciously accepting an unconditional apology, took no further action. It was the first major body-blow to the traditional turf authorities in these islands.

To show how far removed the racing industry was from today, the £336,000, at which the Aga Khan syndicated his French Derby and Grand Prix winner, Charlottesville, was a record price for a syndicated horse.

Already in 1961, Lester had his sights set on the big money in Tote-monopolized France. But the new champion had great hopes at home. That sleek greyhound, Petite Etoile (I'll bet she would never have passed a pre-Olympic sex test for male hormones if she'd been human) was still in training, superbly handled as ever by Lester's retaining trainer, Noel Murless.

Also in the Warren Place stables that spring was a big unraced bay colt by the 1953 Derby winner, Pinza, called Pinturischio. Noel had no doubt about his ability. 'He is definitely a good horse,' he told me. The public had no doubt either. Before he ever saw a racecourse he was quoted at 3 to 1 for the Guineas and 5 to 1 for the Derby — odds which shortened still further after a smooth victory with Lester in the Wood Ditton Stakes. Once again the combination of Murless, Piggott and a good colt was irresistible.

Public opinion and support for 'Pint o'Sherry' forced Noel to go for the gloves in the Guineas though the colt was still too backward and the distance too short.

When Lester drew his whip in the Dip, the big bay favourite found no more and finished fourth behind the 66 to 1 Rockavon, a 420 guineas bargain, the longest-priced Guineas winner in the century and Scotland's first classic hero in living memory.

Despite support for the French colt, Moutiers, a half-brother to the ill-fated Angers, Pinto was still a warm order for the Derby. Looking back now, Lester says: 'He'd have won it all right.'

It was not to be. The nobblers got at him, not once but twice, and on the second occasion they made such a good job of it that they nearly killed him.

Was I so wrong when I wrote in the *Daily Mail* at about this time, just after the death of my old guv'nor, Atty Persse?

'Racing needs more money far more urgently than is generally realized. And this money must come from betting.

'The first racing levy on bookmakers, likely to be made towards the end of next year, is expected to produce an annual £1,250,000. It is an attempt to restore a sick industry to health.

'For racing is sick. Most trainers lose money on ninety-five per cent of their horses. They have to make good their losses by other means.

'Many bookmakers feel that this is the thin end of the wedge because a large section of the racing industry is openly saying that only a Tote monopoly can save racing.

'These people point out that although the increased popularity of National Hunt racing has swelled the estimated total of £350,000,000 gambled every year, our prize-money is ridiculously low and our admission charges fantastically high compared with countries where the Tote reigns supreme.

'One disastrous result is that the English owner seeking our own best bloodstock at Newmarket or Dublin is outbid by foreign rivals.

'When the subject was debated in Parliament the only politician to put his finger on the real problem was Mr Eric Johnson, member for Manchester (Blackley) and nephew of the late and great Atty Persse.

'Persse wrote shortly before he died last year: "I was very proud of my profession twenty-five years ago and I would have been happy to see my son following in his father's footsteps. Today I would do everything in my power to stop him training horses in England."

'In 1939 training fees were five guineas a week. Today owners cannot or will not pay more than ten guineas, although the cost of living has risen four times.

'In the House of Commons, Mr Johnson cited the case of Bruce Hobbs, who, after a successful career as a steeplechase jockey and later as assistant trainer to Cecil Boyd-Rochfort, has decided to join a firm of saddlers rather than set up on his own because ". . . with stakes so small and costs so high, a man cannot be sure of a living unless he bets and wins."

'Mr Johnson commented: "For Bruce Hobbs that was not good enough, and he was quite right."

'So the very foundations of racing are shaky. Tax evasion, betting and dealing are no substitute for a decent living wage.

'To restore the sick industry to health it is essential that owners should get free travel and sufficient prize money to enable them to pay reasonable training fees.

'Until it is worth every trainer's while to run horses on their merits, the ordinary punter will suffer.

'Moreover the new post-war public attracted to the sport by television has been largely repelled by the antiquated, run-down condition of most racecourses.

'And where courses are in this condition it is in spite of the help of increasing Tote grants, course bookmakers' payments and the abolition of entertainment tax.'

Poor Noel had a terrible time trying vainly to overcome the nobblers and prepare his colt for the Derby. The Press didn't help. They knew that there was something wrong that might prevent the favourite from running at Epsom. But, although they were dope-happy at the time, they never suspected the true cause of his mysterious illness.

Under orders from the office, I spent days down at Newmarket with a photographer. Noel was as courteous as he always is at Warren Place, but pictures were not allowed. I remember hiding behind bushes on the heath as the horse was being exercised while my photographer wielded an enormous weapon like a Vickers machine-gun. This was one of two £6,000 cameras then in the possession of the *Daily Mail,* which had been designed for tracking satellites. It was child's play to capture a horse galloping a mile or so away.

Lester says: 'Pinturischio would certainly have won that Derby.'

Noel was one of the first to welcome the Norfolk Committee's report when it finally appeared on 4 May. 'An excellent report — a big advance,' he said.

The most important recommendation was that trainers should no longer be warned off automatically if stopping dope were found in their horses unless it could be proved that they had been involved. It hardly needed great intelligence to work this one out. The rule should never have existed. After all, an elementary knowledge of horses and racing would show that no trainer would ever use drugs to prevent his own horse from winning. There are so many other ways of giving an animal 'an easy' without risking his health or his licence.

Routine tests on at least two winners a day and other horses were ordered by the stewards. Each sample was to be split into three parts, one for a new Jockey Club laboratory, the second for the owner's chosen analyst, and the third to be kept in case of disagreement. The analysts' reports were to be evaluated by an advisory committee of experts before the stewards took any action. These were the main recommendations of this historic document, which at least made a start in righting a grievous wrong.

There were to be no more secret tests. That was very important except for the fact that all stewards' inquiries were still held in secret with no Press and no legal representation for years to come.

The Royal Institute of Chemistry and the Society for Analytical Chemistry had come out strongly against secret tests such as those conducted hitherto by Jockey Club analysts. In a memorandum the chemists said: 'We are strongly opposed to the suggestion that those analysts who make the tests in this country must be members of the American Association of Racecourse Chemists and thereby presumably precluded from stating the methods they use or discussing them with other analysts. We cannot stress sufficiently strongly that nobody should be condemned on secret tests, which cannot be challenged.'

This sort of expert statement, coming on top of the O'Brien case and the apparent injustice of the case of the Irish chaser, Zonda, shattered all the previous ideas of the Jockey Club and their private analysts.

Compelled to take action, no doubt by the Zonda case, the Norfolk Committee insisted that more discretion should be exercised with regard to the disqualification of horses which had been found to be doped. They suggested that the rules should be altered to permit such animals to race again after a maximum suspension of six months.

A cynic might be excused for reflecting that, if the previous June's test of Skymaster after that Ascot race had been official instead of private, the tough Norfolk colt would have been banned for life. He would never have won the Middle Park Stakes and fetched a handsome price before carrying

Scobie Breasley and the second highest weight ever for a three-year-old to victory in the Stewards' Cup.

Trainers were to be warned on their licences that a horse should receive nothing but normal nutrient within a period of seventy-two hours before noon on the day of its race.

Coinciding with the Norfolk report, Vincent O'Brien's suspension ended after twelve instead of eighteen months. His litigation against the Irish Turf Club stewards was still pending.

Meanwhile in France, Elizabeth Couturie's magnificent brown colt, Right Royal V, ridden by Roger Poincelet, was going from strength to strength and, after he had spreadeagled his field in the £35,000 Prix du Jockey Club (French Derby), we looked forward to his clash with four-year-old St Paddy in the Ascot King George VI and Queen Elizabeth Stakes.

Lester, who was, of course, to ride the 1960 Derby winner in the big race, had been seen at his very cheekiest when steering the splendid grey, Petite Etoile, to her second Coronation Cup victory at Epsom. He was not only at his cheekiest but also at his best, because, at five, the 1959 Oaks winner was becoming a little temperamental. She needed kidding, too, and so did the other jockeys. Lester made it look so easy, but he had very little in hand at the end of a mile and a half.

It was one of those starts, which were a disgrace to the sport. This was the Epsom Derby meeting and the race in question was one of the world's classics for older horses. But England still had no starting stalls.

Moreover, Epsom was still in an atrocious state. The ground was not only hard, but appallingly rough so that the tough French challenge of Javelot, winner of the previous year's Eclipse, never materialized. Percy Carter said: 'My horse will never act on such going. If I'd known it was going to be like this, I'd never have brought him.'

This from one of the loyalest expatriate Englishmen, whose jockey, Freddy Palmer, soon discovering the truth of his trainer's words, kept Javelot last all the way round and sensibly made no serious attempt to get on terms.

When the five runners came under orders, Sir Winston Churchill's Vienna charged the starting gate. His jockey, Tommy Gosling, was saved from a crash by the alertness of the starter, Alec Marsh, who released the tapes with a split second to spare, at the same time shouting 'No start' to the other four runners. Vienna went about three hundred yards before returning to the gate.

When they were eventually dispatched, Vienna led from Proud Chieftain. The pace, slow at first, was gradually increased but Lester, lying third, made no move until a furlong from the post. He hardly moved even then but let the filly glide up to the leaders. As she passed Vienna to win by a neck, he still had her on a tight rein.

'It's damn silly,' said a very successful trainer, who once had been a famous jockey. 'If the filly had stumbled slightly she would have lost the race.'

But Noel Murless said happily: 'Knowing her as I do, I was never worried.'

Petite Etoile was running for the first time in the presence of her new owner, the Aga Khan, who had inherited her from his father, Prince Aly Khan, that outstanding judge of racing and racehorses. She had won £65,061, a record for a filly in Britain.

By the time Ascot's July meeting arrived, I had watched all Right Royal's races, including that farcical misjudgment of Roger Poincelet in the Prix de Fontainebleau, when he allowed his pacemaker too much scope and suffered ignominious and unnecessary defeat. Fortunately, of course, the two Couturie runners were coupled for betting purposes, so that the French punters did not lose their francs. So, alone of the so-called experts, I sided firmly with the French champion to beat St Paddy.

In the paddock the big Murless bay, who had dwarfed his rivals before Lester's record-breaking, front-running Eclipse ride the previous Saturday, was now, in his turn, outclassed by Right Royal, who had grown to a powerful 16 hands 3 inches.

The cheer for St Paddy, which started two furlongs out, died to nothing as soon as Roger asked Right Royal for effort. Then the British crowd witnessed what we had seen at Longchamp and Chantilly. The great colt immediately lengthened his stride and swept majestically past St Paddy to win as he liked by three lengths.

His trainer, Etienne Pollet, who was later to handle Sea Bird, declared: 'Nearco is the only horse I have seen in my life as good as Right Royal.'

And Noel said: 'It was no disgrace for St Paddy to be beaten by a horse like that.' The one consolation for British breeders was that Right Royal was a son of our own Hyperion-bred Derby winner, Owen Tudor.

In the same month we saw at Kempton just how brilliant Lester had been throughout Petite Etoile's sensational career. The race was almost designed for her. It was the Aly Khan Memorial Gold Cup and I think that Noel, as one of Aly's oldest friends and greatest admirers, would have given anything to win with the grey mare. But the distance was 1½ miles. This was the flat Kempton circuit and Lester's bluff was called at last. With a superb display of courage and stamina worthy of his great owner, Sir Winston Churchill's High Hat beat the mare fair and square at that evening meeting.

The Aga Khan was perplexed and bewildered at the defeat of his champion, whom he had believed to be the best in the world. 'What happened?' he asked Lester. 'Why didn't you come away and win?'

His head slightly tilted to one side, Lester looked steadily at this dark, handsome young man about his own age. He answered simply: 'He ran me into the ground.'

Walter Nightingall won many races by teaching his horses to make all the running if necessary. Riding to a plan, his jockey, Duncan Keith, jumped off in front and set a fast, true gallop throughout. Lester was still sitting as still as ever on the grey wonder filly two lengths behind. Was his bottom not quite as high in the air as usual?

Two and a half furlongs from home Petite Etoile started to make her move and it looked as though once again she was to sweep by to a — this time — memorably appropriate victory. But it was not to be. Lester urged her on, she got to within a length of High Hat — but could produce no more. Lester gave her a backhander. She shot her bolt and High Hat drew further away to win by two lengths.

I have often thought it would be interesting to take a sex test on those brilliant race-mares. In many cases their head and general bone structure have few feminine characteristics and I wonder whether they possess a preponderance of male hormones. If it's fair and necessary to test women athletes before the Olympic Games, then why not before the Oaks or the Prix Vermeille? We might well find that certain fillies were not entitled to that vital three pounds' allowance in big races like the Arc de Triomphe and the King George VI and Queen Elizabeth Stakes. That allowance *must* be worth about two lengths over a stiff one and a half miles.

The trouble is that our veterinary profession has been falling steadily behind the other leading racing countries. Whereas in America a vet has the status of a doctor and in France the leading vet, Dr Edouard Pouret, was qualified as a doctor before deciding to take up veterinary studies, the English have tended to treat vets as people lower on the social scale.

This is grossly unfair to as fine a bunch of men as you could wish to find anywhere and has had a serious effect on recruitment for the profession. It is only now gradually being overcome. In an industry as important and full of valuable, delicate products the best brains are essential. Veterinary science should be as advanced as medicine instead of lagging behind.

Ironically, of all the great horses that he has ridden, the three which stand out are those on which Lester suffered defeat in his bogey race, the Arc de Triomphe: Sir Ivor, Park Top and Nijinsky.

Lester now inclines to the view that Sir Ivor was the best horse he has ever ridden. 'Crepello was a very good horse,' he says. 'I don't think we ever saw the best of him because of his legs. I think he was better than he showed.' Crepello, who won the Guineas and Derby in 1957, was as bold and brave with his mares at the Eve Stud as he was on the racecourse.

That was the year when Lester and Noel also won the Oaks for the Queen with Carrozza by a short head from Silken Glider, ridden by Jimmy Eddery, whose son Pat is one of our finest riders today. 'Carrozza was only a pony,' says Lester, 'but as game as a pebble. I was a bit lucky. I got up on the inside. The second would have beaten me in another stride. My filly had done everything.' This was, in fact, one of the most brilliant feats of jockeymanship I have ever seen, as Gordon commented earlier in this chapter.

From the moment that he arrived at Ballydoyle as a year-ling in the autumn of 1966 Sir Ivor was looked on as something special by that genius of trainers, Vincent O'Brien. The handsome bay son of Sir Gaylord had everything you look for in a really high-class horse, combining power and grace of body and action with a lovely, intelligent, all-male head and the boldest outlook, which gave him the most tremendous personality and presence.

He had already won his only two races, including the National Stakes at The Curragh when Vincent took him to Longchamp for Lester to ride in Europe's most valuable two-year-old race, the £32,000 Grand Criterium. In this traditionally all-French contest — which, like Phil Bull's brainchild, the *Timeform* Gold Cup, seldom tells a lie — Sir Ivor fairly spreadeagled the best two-year-olds in France.

In the spring of 1968 Vincent revealed that the colt had actually grown two inches during the winter and now stood 16 hands 2 inches. As we watched him work, his trainer said proudly: 'Whatever he does, he is a truly magnificent specimen of the thoroughbred. He's on his toes, too. Last year he was like an old sheep. Now he can really jump and kick.'

Watching Sir Ivor's smooth, daisy-cutting action as he cantered up the sawdust gallop behind his lead horse, Missile — third in the 1967 Guineas — I marvelled at his superb development. I had never seen such an impressive classic prospect.

Lester was in an enviable position. He could choose between Sir Ivor and the top English colt, Petingo, on whom he had won the Gimcrack for his father-in-law, Sam Armstrong. This brilliantly fast, rich bay son of Petition with the distinctive white face and hind socks, now stood 15 hands 3½ inches. He had lengthened into a shape which might not please the purist but which epitomized power and produced the action of a perfectly oiled machine. Clearly on his breeding he would not stay the Derby distance. Nor would he be asked to do so.

His rival, on the other hand, had always been earmarked for Epsom. There was never any real doubt, therefore, about Lester's decision and, on 17 March when he announced that he would ride Sir Ivor, the American colt was already 5 to 2 for the Guineas and 5 to 1 for the Derby.

He was 6 to 4 for the first classic after he had won Ascot's Two Thousand Guineas Trial comfortably by half a length in a time nearly half a second faster than the average for the track, despite the earliness of the season. It was only 5 April.

As in the Grand Criterium, Sir Ivor showed that he possessed three essential qualities: he could settle, accelerate and had the killer instinct. The massive colt, drawn on the outside

of seven runners, cut his tongue as he hit his mouth on the
stalls — he had done the same at The Curragh — and was last
away. Inside the last two furlongs Lester let the 15 to 8 on
favourite sweep smoothly past his field. But he had to shake
him up to resist Bill Williamson's typical opportunist dash
on Dalry.

Vincent said: 'When he heard the other horse coming, my
fellow quickened instinctively to win. I was very pleased with
him.'

Lester was genuinely enthusiastic. 'I wish we had ten more
like him,' he said.

To which Vincent quietly replied: 'If I had one as good,
I'd be more than satisfied.'

Nevertheless, the Newmarket horses were so forward in
condition that season that they were sweeping the board and
a few days later the American colt drifted to 2 to 1, while
Petingo shortened to 11 to 4. And when, ridden by Joe
Mercer, the latter made all his own running to win the Craven
Stakes over the Guineas course and distance, the positions in
the market were reversed. Petingo became favourite at 7 to 4,
while Sir Ivor went out to 5 to 2.

It's strange to look back. Sir Cecil Boyd-Rochfort, watching Petingo being unsaddled, said: 'That's the one I'd want to
be on. I wish he were mine.'

Greek shipowner Marcos Lemos, whose colt he was,
revealed that he had turned down a million dollars for his
unbeaten star during the winter. 'I'll sell ships,' he said, 'but I
won't sell Petingo. Socrates believed fame was more important
than money.' Clearly, as one of the last and best of Petition's
stock, the colt was already worth more than this figure as a
stallion.

The initial phase of the Newmarket face-lift was well under
way. The expenditure of £600,000 had been severely
criticized, but racing must have a suitable headquarters and
this excellent compromise — involving the complete moderni-
zation of the solid old stands, a change in layout behind them
and the democratization of the whole — has proved an outstanding success.

When May Day 1968 arrived, Sir Ivor had returned to
favouritism at 11 to 8 and Petingo had retreated to 9 to 4.
The market was fully justified when Lester's mount won in
the style of a true champion. His rival, however, ran an excel-

lent race to finish second 1½ lengths away and 2½ lengths in front of Jimmy Reppin. Time was to show that this was a very good Guineas indeed.

Now Sir Ivor was naturally a strong favourite for the Derby and, in spite of an excellent gallop by Connaught with the previous year's winner, Royal Palace, he started at 5 to 4 on to become the shortest-priced winner since Cicero, 11 to 4 on, in 1905.

Revelling in brilliant sunshine, an enormous crowd saw the perfect judgment of Britain's champion jockey and the supreme skill of a great Irish trainer win the Derby for the United States. Class characterized the whole performance.

In the parade the favourite stood out as a superb, sleek, perfectly trained thoroughbred, towering above his rivals as he jumped and kicked with well-being. Burly, temperamental Connaught, though sweating a little, went straight into the stalls and the remainder followed quickly.

Blinkered Benoy, ridden by Duncan Keith, jumped off in front and led at the top of the hill, followed by Connaught, Laureate, Society, Atopolis, Remand and Sir Ivor. Half-way down the hill Sandy Barclay sent Connaught into the lead in front of Laureate with Society close up third. At this stage Lester had Sir Ivor on the rails inside Mount Athos.

Now Sandy, handling his big mount with outstanding horsemanship, adopted the only possible tactics. He made his best way home. Lester, however, had faith in Sir Ivor. He did not move, until a furlong and a half out. Then we saw the big horse's fantastic acceleration. He flew up the hill to overhaul the leader close to home and win, apparently still barely extended, by a length and a half.

Sandy said: 'I thought Sir Ivor wouldn't stay, but when I saw him there half a furlong out, although my chap was running on, I knew that we'd made it. He's the most brilliant horse I have ever seen — in all my nineteen years!'

This opinion was — and still is — shared by the winner's thirty-one-year-old jockey, who was winning his fourth Derby. 'It was over in a few strides,' said Lester. 'I didn't ask him to do anything until one and a half furlongs out. He was always going well and never gave a moment's anxiety. Sir Ivor is the best horse I have ever ridden.' Again this was to prove him right, as the form unfolded to demonstrate the true worth of this Derby.

Lester says: 'He's a really great horse and a wonderful character. But he didn't get more than 1¼ miles.' Only he really knew this. As with Petite Etoile and so many other non-stayers, Lester had brilliantly held his colt up, delivered his challenge with split-second timing and made it look easy on the track where, despite its vaunted tradition for being the most testing course in the world, a short-runner can triumph.

So he was far from worried when Vincent's stable-jockey, that magnificent horseman and delightful character Liam Ward, took over the colt at The Curragh for the Irish Sweeps Derby. Liam was under contract to ride the O'Brien horses in Ireland, although the Ballydoyle trainer was free to engage any other rider, such as Lester, for his runners abroad.

So Lester, knowing that Sir Ivor's stamina would be much more severely tested on the stiff galloping course of The Curragh with its long, hard pull up to the finish, was happy to accept the ride on Charles Engelhard's tough, plain bay Ribot colt, Ribero, trained by young Fulke Johnson-Houghton at Blewbury.

A few days before this wonderfully-organized race, which has now become one of the world's great classics, half of Vincent's horses were stricken with a mild infection, but Sir Ivor, who had been isolated, escaped and was in great form to justify the faith of his many supporters. I wrote from Dublin:

'Sir Ivor will bring his earnings to £173,557 if winning the Irish Sweeps Derby in the United States on rain-softened turf at The Curragh this afternoon.

'Many visitors, including your correspondent, were prevented from landing at Dublin yesterday owing to heavy rain and mist, and were redirected to Belfast, but the going is expected to be just on the soft side of good.

'There is never a certainty in racing. But, barring a stroke of cruel fate such as crippled Relko before this race, or the sudden infection of his stablemates' virus, the big, handsome bay is the nearest thing since Arkle in his Cheltenham Gold Cups.

'Moreover the favourite was heavily backed yesterday with inspired money at the prohibitive odds of 2 to 1 on and is likely to start still shorter.

'You can back his rivals three ways with Ladbrokes — at starting price, or without the favourite, or to be second to Sir

Ivor. But if you back an outsider each way with the favourite at odds-on you will get no better than 3 to 1 a place.

'I understand that bookmakers have helped to balance their books by investing in sweep tickets, but William Hill says Sir Ivor has ruined Sweeps Derby as a betting proposition. Our field money on the race is 66 per cent down on 1967.

'There were some doubts about Sir Ivor's stamina before his brilliant speed for the final dramatic burst.

'But Vincent O'Brien says: "Now that we know he gets the trip, its so much easier. We won't need to hold him up like that." And thirty-eight-year-old Liam Ward, one of the world's most accomplished jockeys, knows this stiff Curragh track even better than Piggott knows Epsom.

'Although La Lagune won the Oaks, there were no French challengers for the Epsom Derby, so that this afternoon's clash will provide the year's first guide to the classic form of the colts in the three countries.

'While there are three English runners, the French should surely win the battle for second place, with the only other genuine classic colt in the event, Val d'Aoste, who ran a great race to finish third in the French Derby.'

How wrong you can be. Poor Liam. Sir Ivor, done with after 1¼ miles, struggled on unhappily and scrambled into second place behind Ribero, on whose stable-companion Ribocco Lester had won the previous year. He finished so distressed that Vincent thought he must have caught the virus, which had threatened his preparation. 'His galloping companion, Ballygoran, who was isolated with him, caught it two days ago,' he said. But the day after the race he reported: 'Sir Ivor appears to be very well and none the worse for his race.'

Lester had been widely criticized for his riding of the colt at Epsom and for leaving his effort so late that he did not take the lead until fifty yards from the post. He was now completely vindicated, although many of the critics insisted that Sir Ivor had got the trip all right and directed their barbs at Liam. 'Change the jockeys and you'd change the result,' they said.

Now Raymond Guest, the giant former international polo star, who was currently American ambassador to Ireland, decided to aim Sir Ivor for the Eclipse, taking on not only

Royal Palace, who had won the Coronation Cup most impressively, but also the French colt Taj Dewan.

Lester says: 'He was wrong in himself and he was never striding out. Royal Palace was a good, but lucky, horse. Everything went right for him. Even when he broke down at Ascot it was right on the line!'

Owner and trainer decided to rest Sir Ivor now for an autumn campaign with the Arc de Triomphe as their objective. So Lester resumed his partnership with Ribero in the St Leger. I have always believed that he rode the race of his life in the Doncaster classic run over 1 mile 6 furlongs 132 yards on a colt, who just did not get the trip. He displayed superb artistry, sitting and suffering when Bill Williamson challenged on Canterbury in the final furlong, for Ribero was out on his feet. Yet somehow they held on to win by a short head.

David McCall, Charles Engelhard's racing manager, whose charm is matched only by his skill and knowledge of every phase of racing and breeding, said: 'It's fantastic how any jockey could stay so cool. Ribero died in Lester's hand after 1¾ miles, but somehow he kept him going for the extra 132 yards.'

Neither the slow time of 3 minutes 19.8 seconds — it was the worst of the century — nor the closeness of the finish detracted in any way from the triumph of the late Charles Engelhard, the platinum king, who was Ian Fleming's friend and model for Goldfinger (the character in his book of the same name), and of his twenty-eight-year-old trainer, Fulke Johnson-Houghton. They had won both the Irish Sweeps Derby and the Leger with two full-brothers by Ribot out of the British mare Libra in successive years.

Now all attention was focused on the Arc de Triomphe, already worth £83,400 to the winner. Sir Ivor, rested, came back to the track at Longchamp after two months' absence and, giving the winner 9 lbs, was beaten half a length by Prince Sao in the 11 furlong Prix Henri Delamarre. He went out to 10 to 1 for the Arc, although on several lines of form the result was fairly predictable after his lay-off. Vaguely Noble, was, of course, hot favourite at 3 to 1.

That splendid colt duly won, and Lester commented: 'I was always with the winner, but he was pulling over me all the time. That's the best race Sir Ivor has ever run.' The answer was, of course, that, whereas Vaguely Noble stayed every inch of 1½ miles, Sir Ivor did not.

Two days later that brilliant, indefatigable story-hunter Peter O'Sullevan, who had spoken to Vincent, wrote in the *Daily Express* that Sir Ivor would never race again, but would be retired to stud.

Every racing journalist in England seems to find his way to the Arc de Triomphe, which is always a huge bun-fight and, of course, a one-day wonder. Very few, however, find their way back to Longchamp the following Sunday when the Grand Criterium is run. To me there is no comparison. The Criterium is far more exciting because it is the future. Here are the classic contenders for next year doing battle for a wonderful prize.

So, as usual, I flew out after racing in England on Saturday. At Longchamp on Sunday I met Sir Ivor's owner, whom I have known well for some years. 'What's the matter, Raymond?' I asked. 'Is your horse sick?'

'No, Vincent tells me he's as fit as a fiddle.'

'Then why on earth are you, of all people, backing down from the Champion and the Washington International? I'll never believe that Raymond Guest is too scared to accept a challenge. You've got them at your mercy.'

It had the desired effect on the grand, silver-haired sportsman. That evening I hurried back to my hotel to file an exclusive story for the *Daily Mail*.

'The Derby winner, Sir Ivor, is not to retire after all.

'He will run in the Champion Stakes at Newmarket on Saturday, and is quite likely to go for the Washington International on 11 November.

'On the eve of his departure for the United States, the colt's owner, Raymond Guest, said at Longchamp today: "He is definitely running at Newmarket and we are thinking about taking on Damascus at Laurel. I'm not going to say 'No' to anything."

'Lester Piggott will ride Sir Ivor, who returned to his best form when second in the Prix de l'Arc de Triomphe, and who will be ideally suited by both the stiff Newmarket 1¼ miles, and the easy 1½ miles of the International.

'A unique confrontation between the Derby and Oaks winners may now occur at Laurel Park. François Boutin said that La Lagune is definitely running. "I would like to have her run in the Champion," he says, "but her owner particularly wants to go for the International." '

The Champion Stakes fell like a ripe plum into Vincent's lap. Sir Ivor, appreciating the return to his best distance of a mile and a quarter, won with impressive ease. The Washington International must surely be his, if only he could stay the 1½ miles as he had done in the Derby.

For those of us who visit the United States just once a year, and that only if we are lucky, the trip to Laurel is an adventure. John Schapiro is not only a wonderful organizer, but a most fabulous host. At last he was seeing the realization of a dream, which had started in 1952 when, always a realist, he inaugurated this United Nations of racing on the famous Maryland circuit which his father and he had acquired. The winner of the English Derby, still recognized as the most famous traditional race in the world, was included in the field for the Washington International.

Tired, as always, from the long flight and the unaccustomed change in time, Vincent and I, friends of long standing before I dreamt of becoming a journalist, dined together in the restaurant of the motel where we were staying, waited on by girls in black leather miniskirts, who looked sexy enough in the dark, pink-lighted, smoke-laden atmosphere, but whom daylight might not have treated so kindly. It was ten o'clock. We were trying to forget that at home we would by now have been in bed fast asleep for at least four hours. Vincent was very worried about his horse's lack of work since the Champion, but he remained his cool, charming self, even when an apparently drunk, burly man in a loud check jacket lurched into our table.

Our sozzled newcomer did not bother to introduce himself. He glared at Vincent. 'I know you,' he said. 'You're a trainer from England. Let's see. Murless, isn't it?'

I opened my mouth to correct the error, but Vincent, saying nothing, shook his head slightly in discouragement. Europe's most famous trainer, who had already brought the favourite to Laurel, was not to be drawn.

'I got it. You're Prendergast, aren't you?'

Vincent smiled. 'I often wish I was,' he said. 'He's a wonderful trainer.'

'Well, well, then you've got to be O'Brien. Vincent O'Brien, isn't it? You came here with Ballymoss and got beat.'

A slight nod and the Tipperary trainer carried on with his meal.

'Now tell me about this horse of yours. He's a big colt. Bigger than Ballymoss, huh? And Ballymoss was beaten by the sharp track.'

Silence.

'Wouldn't you say this track is a damned sight too sharp for a fine leg colt like Sir Ivor?'

'No,' said Vincent. 'I wouldn't. I think the course is in wonderful shape. And I never said it was too sharp for Ballymoss. You said that.'

Our new 'friend', disgruntled, left without another word.

Vincent said: 'That chap knows me very well. He's a leading racecourse columnist called ＿＿＿＿＿＿＿＿. All he was trying to do was to get me to criticize the course in any way. Then you'd see the headlines tomorrow — "O'Brien slams Laurel!" And that wouldn't be fair on anyone, least of all on John Schapiro.'

The little Cork man, who had already produced three successive Grand National winners and won two Derbys, told me that Sir Ivor had been unable to leave his box from the time of the Champion Stakes at Newmarket until he flew over to Laurel.

'A little gravel worked its way up into his hoof and he was as lame as a cat,' he said. 'I poulticed him myself night and morning to get him sound, but he had done nothing at all when he left for Laurel.'

As a result Sir Ivor had to be worked on successive days in order to clear his wind. The American turf-writers all wrote that O'Brien was giving his horse too much galloping.

Unlike the previous year, when Ribocco was beaten out of sight in a typical Maryland Indian summer, the weather was colder and more wintry than in the England we had left behind.

Vincent did, in fact, confide: 'The course was too sharp for Ballymoss and I'm afraid it may be the same for Sir Ivor. However, not only is he smaller than both Kelso and Mungo, who each won the International, but, like them, he is bred for American circuits.'

Moreover since Ballymoss's years the course had been considerably improved. It had been banked very skilfully, so that it no longer resembled a flat Newton Abbott and it had a good, solid covering of grass, which in the previous year's dry spell had had to be sprayed green!

It is all so different from English racing that I am reprinting the articles that I filed from Laurel in this our greatest year with the best horse we have ever sent from these islands to compete in the Washington International.

Laurel (Maryland), Thursday
'A bare-back rider galloping a big-race candidate enlivened this morning's scene at Laurel Park, where a night of steady rain has just removed the last obstacle to Sir Ivor's triumph on Monday.

'Vincent O'Brien, who said on arrival: "The Laurel course is excellent — you won't find a better grass track anywhere", was even more enthusiastic as we watched Sir Ivor at work. "The rain is just what the doctor ordered for my horse," he said. "The ground should be perfect."

'The 11 to 10 favourite for the £42,000 Washington International is eating well and has even put on weight, despite the 3,500-mile journey from Tipperary. "He slept most of the way," said travelling headman Maurice O'Callaghan, who brought sufficient plastic containers of Tipperary water for Sir Ivor and his lead horse, Ballygoran.

'Local pundits enthused about the Derby winner's condition as he walked on to the track, ridden by newly-wed jockey Vincent Rossiter.

'Led eight lengths by Ballygoran, Sir Ivor galloped five furlongs down the back stretch, round the bend and up past the finish. Unbalanced coming into the turn, he changed legs happily and, when Rossiter asked him, simply flew past the leader.

'Even O'Brien gasped. "He just eats him," he said. Then, as the big bay came back, his trainer noticed that he was blowing a little. "That's just what he wanted. He'll probably do the same tomorrow."

'Starter Eddie Blind is satisfied with Sir Ivor, and will not test him through the barrier. "Lester Piggott and the horse know enough about it for me," he said.

'Monday's field had now been whittled down to eight probables, all of whom have now arrived. Last year's winner, Fort Marcy, came in from New York today.

'Absentees are the Brazilian Derby winner, Sabinus, who refused to return to his aircraft after a stop in Rio, and the

Peruvian Trastevere whose papers were held up by a local revolution.

'Tiny British-bred Czar Alexander — barely 15 hands 3 inches — worked five furlongs in fractionally faster time than Sir Ivor.

' "I'm pleased," said his trainer, Angel Penna. "He did it easily and we didn't push him too hard."

'Oaks winner La Lagune looked and moved really well on the dirt track, so familiar to a Chantilly-trained animal, but was not given serious work.

'Her countryman, Carmarthen, however, the tall, leggy French chestnut who finished third to Vaguely Noble and Sir Ivor in the Arc, comes from the Strassburger stable which had won the 1953 International with Worden.

'His trainer, Lucien Baldisseri, said: "Another furlong and I'd have beaten Sir Ivor at Longchamp." This big horse may find this track too sharp.

'Petrone, last of the French trio, has just arrived and was given walking exercise, but Japan's Takeshiba-O, sired by the Blagrave horse China Rock, went through the starting-gate before working, his tail plaited against the mud.

'The most unusual sight of all, however, was the saddle-less Argentinian Azincourt, who galloped twice round with work-jockey Nicholas Pisano.'

Laurel (Maryland), Friday
'Lester Piggott's decision to challenge the English weather by riding at Haydock tomorrow before flying to Baltimore has flabbergasted the Americans.

'They say: "With millions of pounds depending on the result how can he possibly risk it all for a £5,000 race?"

'The British champion, however, is so confident of getting here by Saturday evening that Vincent O'Brien has no jockey standing by.

' "I am expecting Lester to be riding Sir Ivor out on the track on Sunday morning," he said.

'The Derby winner was allotted No. 6 in the eight-horse field, to the satisfaction of his trainer, when for the second year I was one of the guests invited to make the draw at a lavish breakfast ceremony.

'Czar Alexander is drawn 4, Fort Marcy 8, and the Oaks winner, La Lagune, 7.

'Sir Ivor showed his appreciation of the Laurel turf when the skies cleared at last this morning. He breezed five furlongs in 1 minute 23.5 seconds, on a tight rein, and then lashing out with sheer high spirits, missed a British journalist's head by an inch.

'The big bay colt stormed past Ballygoran and pulled up in two strides. With Vincent O'Brien I ran to listen to his breathing. He would not have blown a candle out. "I don't believe he could be any fitter," his trainer said.

'Local horses are ridden round the track by coloured stable-lads, whose short stirrup leathers make Piggott look like a policeman.

'No races will be run on the grass circuit before the International which will start at about 10.15 p.m. British time on Monday.

'François Boutin, trainer of La Lagune, has arrived on his first visit to America accompanied by his jockey, Gerard Thiboeuf. Once again according to the eminently successful French tradition, the Oaks winner only cantered, freshening up for the big day.

'It is becoming increasingly clear that, provided the ground dries up, the bay filly is the one real danger to the favourite. She showed in the Arc that she is coming to her best, and she is the only other true classic animal in the field. She will start at a long price.

'Fort Marcy, last year's winner, galloped a circuit of the track on the dirt, and will work five furlongs on the grass tomorrow.

'British-bred Czar Alexander was "ponied"! That is to say he was led round riderless at a slow canter by an exercise boy, colourfully dressed and riding one of the many ponies on the track.

'American experts believe that Sir Ivor will not start favourite. It is expected that Czar Alexander, who won the Man o'War so impressively, will be made favourite, and that his victim on that occasion, Fort Marcy, will perhaps be preferred to Sir Ivor.

'The Argentinian Azincourt, once again ridden bare-back, galloped at half-speed twice round the circuit. The Japanese candidate, Takeshiba-O, worked again. From the amount of galloping he has done, there will be precious little left of him by Monday.

Laurel (Maryland), Sunday

'Snow and slush greeted Lester Piggott as he arrived at the track this morning to ride Sir Ivor in the final race-winning blow-out for tomorrow's Washington International.

'Local rumours about his well-being were quickly dispelled, and the big bay nostrils never quivered when he pulled up. As we paddled through the mud Vincent O'Brien said: "He's as fit as he can be. I am very happy about everything. The going will not be as heavy as at Longchamp last month."

'And since travelling headman Maurice O'Callaghan reports the horse as "just perfect" Raymond Guest's courageous gamble will surely pay off in a triumphant boost for British racing by the even-money favourite.

'Oaks winner La Lagune, who slaughtered the Arc de Triomphe third, Carmarthen, over five furlongs on Saturday, should finish second in this historic clash of an Epsom classic pair. At 12 to 1 she looks fair value.

'But her trainer, François Boutin, says: "I think the ground is too heavy for her." After the race she is off to stud in Florida.

'British-bred Czar Alexander has a good record on soft going, and at 4 to 1 is probably the chief danger to Sir Ivor.

'The little bay impressed shivering watchers in the rain, including the British contingent, with a fast three-furlong spin, clocking 37.4 seconds on a tight rein.

'Last year's winner, Fort Marcy, and the Argentinian Azincourt, who has been backed from 100 to 1 down to 20 to 1, were given walking exercise.

'Elliott Burch, trainer of Fort Marcy, said: "Racing is like show business. You are as good as your last performance", emphasizing that the recent form of Paul Mellon's four-year-old has not been that of a big-race winner. He was beaten four lengths behind Czar Alexander in the Man o'War Stakes.

'Connections claim that Takeshiba-O is the best three-year-old in Japan and, indeed, the best horse that country has sent over for the race, but the hard-working bay does not look good enough.

'Azincourt, now owned by American Bert Firestone, is clearly a good strong five-year-old just below classic form.

'Australian Bill Pyers, wearing a pale blue and brown check Balmoral bonnet complete with pompom, rode Petrone in a three-furlong spin.

'While agreeing with her trainer, Maurice Zilber, that the brown four-year-old, a tough improving sort, will run well, I fancy that the going will be too soft for him. And Carmarthen, the tall French chestnut, does not appreciate the turf.

'Prize money of £62,500 is distributed right down for the first five places. It will be the seventeenth running of this ambitious promotion.

'Further rain to disperse the snow is forecast for today, and drier weather tomorrow, but with a temperature of only 40°F. What a good thing that the entire stand is covered in with glass and centrally heated!

'It is a very different world, but one which Sir Ivor, the best horse ever sent from England and Ireland, and British champion jockey Lester Piggott, are all set to conquer tomorrow.'

Laurel (Maryland), Monday

'Lester Piggott rode the race of his life to win the Washington International on the English Derby winner, Sir Ivor, and realize John Schapiro's dream of international racing.

'The British champion jockey, showing the cool cheek of a great horseman, overcame all difficulties and pounced in the last fifty yards to win by three-quarters of a length from the American favourite, Czar Alexander, at the remarkable odds of nearly 2 to 1.

'Master-trainer Vincent O'Brien said to his American rival, Angel Penna: "Sorry you had to come second."

' "Sir Ivor is a super horse. He was in difficulties all the way round. Once he got the opening, then, ping! This is the best horse I've ever trained."

'Takeshiba-O led for the first half-mile in front of Czar Alexander, with Fort Marcy third, Petrone fourth, and Sir Ivor sixth on the rails.

'At the mile post the Japanese colt fell back, yielding to Czar Alexander who then disputed the lead with his countryman, Fort Marcy, last year's winner, ridden by Manuel Yeza, winner of his only three internationals.

'At this stage Sir Ivor had actually dropped back to last place, but in two furlongs, while the leading pair remained the same, with Carmarthen now third, the favourite had moved into fourth position.

'But he still appeared to be hopelessly shut in.

'As they turned into the short straight, Piggott got his mount balanced and slipped through in the last fifty yards to win decisively by three-quarters of a length from Czar Alexander with Fort Marcy a head away third.

'Carmarthen was 1¼ lengths away fourth, La Lagune fifth, Petrone sixth, Azincourt seventh and Takeshiba-O last.

'Piggott said: "If the ground had not been so soft I could have won by 100 yards. When I shook him into action I knew I would win."

' "I had a little trouble getting through."

'The winning owner, Raymond Guest, lost one of his contact lenses on his way to the unsaddling enclosure.

' "This is my lucky day though," he said. "I am so delighted. I was a bit scared all the way. It was very close."

'Sir Ivor will now return to Ireland to stand at stud for one season available to British breeders as a special gesture from Guest, the former international polo player, who has just completed four years as American Ambassador to Ireland. The horse will then return to the United States.

'None of Sir Ivor's opponents had any valid excuses. British Derby form has now been boosted sky-high.

'O'Brien said: "I must pay tribute to the efforts of John Schapiro to bring together these horses for this race." '

On the same day that my piece appeared in London the American papers published the most vitriolic reports, criticizing Lester's riding of the winner in the most vicious way, even referring to him as a 'bum'. Of course they were unfamiliar with his style, so different from any that they were accustomed to, and wrote in complete ignorance of the difficulties with which he was faced. Trying to hold up a brilliant, unfit, big non-stayer, who would stop when he hit the front, in a moderate field, so that he would get a mile and a half was the problem which only Lester could solve.

Looking back now and thinking of this wonderful horse, whom he grew to love, Lester says, 'I have never known a horse so tired as Sir Ivor after that American race. They go flat out for the last mile. That is why their horses are so hard to beat.'

Horse and rider had given their all and he resented the venomous critics bitterly. Quite apart from the fact that he had won, it was, after all, an invitation race and he was a guest in their country.

In the words of the old saying, however, 'there's always another day in racing'. It came for Lester next year when he won again on Lord Iveagh's grand colt, Karabas, trained by Bernard van Cutsem.

A columnist in the *Washington Post* described the British champion's post-race treatment of him and his colleagues: 'On entering the jockeys' room, Piggott shouted: "I'm not saying anything to you guys after what you wrote about me last year. Just clear the hell out!"' '

In fact the words used were quite a bit stronger! But the chief writer in the same paper, under the headline, 'Piggott silences the critics with Karabas', said his performance was a 'masterful ride'.

Under the expert guidance of Richard Baerlein they made a glorious film entitled *The Year of Sir Ivor*. It is the best film ever produced about racing, in keeping with its subject — the greatest horse of the post-war era.

Raymond announced that his horse would begin stud duties in Ireland for the benefit of breeders in these islands, as a measure of his gratitude for the kindness he had received over here. There was, however, consternation and some bitterness when he decided on an American-size stud-fee of £8,000 — nearly three times the then highest European figure. On the usual ration of forty mares a year this represented an income of £320,000. Nevertheless within a week the list was full, and the bluest-blooded mares on this side of the Atlantic were being booked for Sir Ivor's services at Raymond's Ballygoran Stud in Co. Dublin. As his own contribution to the harem the owner paid a European record price to acquire the brilliant Hula Dancer at Deauville.

Then the tug-of-war started. American interests, headed by Bull Hancock, applied the strongest pressure to persuade Raymond to transfer Sir Ivor to Kentucky. The result was inevitable.

A spokesman for Ballygoran told me in March 1970: 'Mr Guest is in a very difficult position as the man in the middle of this tug-of-war, and he can't make up his mind. He promised to send Sir Ivor to Bull Hancock some time ago, and Bull is anxious to have the horse right away. But all the people over here in Ireland and England are trying to persuade him to stay. We need him badly. He will be just one of twenty-six stallions at Hancock's Claiborne Farm. If we could only keep him here for another five years, it wouldn't be so bad. His foals are lovely.' They were indeed and from the moment that they first appeared on the open market it was clear that Sir Ivor was going to dominate the sales as he had the race-track. His departure at the end of the 1970 covering season was a tragedy for British breeding.

Of Nijinsky, the superb Engelhard Triple Crown winner, Lester says: 'He was a brilliant racehorse, of course, but he was highly strung. He always seemed to be looking at birds. He hadn't Sir Ivor's character.'

He enthuses over the Duke of Devonshire's 500 guinea bargain mare, Park Top, who was so splendidly handled by Bernard van Cutsem. 'She was a marvellous mare,' says Lester. 'Undoubtedly she was far better if she didn't have to lie up and could be held up for a late run. You can't do that in a race like the Arc. Even if I hadn't left it too late, Levmoss might well have found more.'

He doesn't like riding on the dirt tracks of America. 'It's terrible to ride on. It's like someone hurling sand at you. You come back with red marks all over your body. The first time I wondered what on earth had happened. English horses won't face it the first two or three times they run over there. I don't blame them!'

One of the momentous and far-reaching events in Lester's life – and in racing generally – was his break with Sir Noel Murless in May 1966 after a ten years' partnership which produced two Derbys, two Oaks and two St Legers. Since Lester had taken over from Gordon as first jockey to Warren Place, Noel had headed the trainers' list four times, and Lester had won three jockeys' championships.

The retainer system had become so traditional a part of the English racing scene that the very idea of a break was a tremendous shock to everyone. Lester came in for such a lot of harsh criticism that it is only fair to let him tell his own version of the events which the public first heard of in my *Daily Mail* story of 18 May, just nine days before the Oaks, for which Charles Clore's Irish One Thousand Guineas winner, Valoris, a half-sister to the French Derby winner, Val de Loir, trained by Vincent O'Brien, was favourite.

Long before 1966 Lester had been toying with the idea of

giving up his £2,000 a year retainer — 'It wasn't much, was it?' — and going freelance. He makes no bones of his admiration for Noel: 'A wonderful trainer, equally good with colts and fillies. A great man at his job.' But he found him a difficult character to deal with sometimes.

For a long time Lester kept quiet in face of all criticism. 'Loyalty', said Gordon Richards, 'is the essence of racing. When Steve Donoghue was offered all those Derby rides, gave up his retainer and turned freelance, I took over as first jockey to Fred Darling. I also took over the jockeys' championship from him.'

Now nine-times champion Lester defends himself:

'This is the true story', he says 'of what happened in that break-up.'

'I told Noel towards the end of 1965 that I had decided to go freelance next season. He tried to dissuade me, but I was determined and, when I refused to accept the retainer for the first time, he must have realized that I was serious. Certainly we carried on as though nothing had happened, but I knew things were bound to come to a head sooner or later.

'This was Charlottown's year, the year when French visitors were banned owing to swamp fever, a year when Noel had some moderate horses at Warren Place.

'Since he had no classic colt worthy of the name, I had been booked for Charles Engelhard's big black Right Noble in the Derby. A soft, disappointing animal, who was often likened to a Life Guards' charger, he was trained by Vincent O'Brien.

'Vincent is a brilliant trainer. Anyone who can saddle three consecutive Grand National winners and five Derby winners, quite apart from all the others, must be quite outstanding.

'He had won the Oaks the previous year, with Long Look. This time in the fillies' classic he had a half-sister to the French Derby winner, Val de Loir, called Valoris; Vincent's brother Dermot and Alan Clore had bought her at Deauville Sales as a yearling for £11,000 on behalf of the latter's father, Sir Charles Clore.

'Since she had a late-maturing pedigree, Vincent didn't train her seriously before she won the Irish One Thousand Guineas. He had given her all the time she wanted. After that race at The Curragh we decided that she probably was a very good filly indeed, who would be worth a great deal of money if she won the Oaks at Epsom.

'And what was to beat her? Noel had a filly called Varinia, who was a fair performer, but just not in the same class. And Vincent really knew the time of day with fillies that year. He had won the One Thousand Guineas at Newmarket too, with Glad Rags.

'I had won the Chester Cup on that splendid tough stayer Aegean Blue and wanted to ride him again in the big race at Ayr on Saturday, 14 May.

'This was the day, however, when Varinia was due to run in the Oaks Trial at Lingfield. Noel let me off and put Stan Clayton up on his filly, who duly won. Incidentally I broke the course record on Aegean Blue at Ayr. I hinted to the Press that weekend that I might not be on Varinia in the Oaks.

'Noel unhappily seemed to take it for granted that I was still stable-jockey even though he was not paying me a retainer and that I would automatically ride his filly at Epsom on 27 May. He announced: "I told Piggott on Sunday that Varinia would run in the Oaks and that I would require him to ride her. As far as I am concerned, he will be on my filly."

'In fact when he said that to me, I replied: "Stan won on her yesterday. He can ride her again." He had no claim on me at all.

'But he decided to bring matters to a head. So I told him that I had accepted the ride on Valoris. I was very sorry he took it as he did. It could have been a perfectly friendly agreement.

'But habit dies hard and big English trainers like Noel had always been accustomed to having their stable-jockeys riding the horses both in their home-work and on the racecourse. The whole thing was a shock to him. It upset all his arrangements and disturbed his way of life. The papers made a sensation of it.

'Vincent broke the news officially when he announced that I would ride for him in all three big Epsom races: the Derby, the Coronation Cup and the Oaks.

'The first two were disappointing. Right Noble, great gangling thing that he was — a caricature of his sire Right Royal — sprawled badly down the hill, while in the Coronation Cup Donato failed to reach the first four.

'My judgment proved right, however, when I won my third Oaks on Valoris, who had been installed favourite at 11 to 10.

'It would have been ironical indeed and would have delighted my many critics if I had been parted from Valoris before the race. I wonder how many officials would have bothered to catch her! It so nearly happened.

'Trained to the minute and looking superb, she was shying so badly that I took her back to the paddock and dismounted. Then, accompanied by Vincent's headman, I led Valoris all the way through the crowds down the hill and up the other side to the start.

'Stan Clayton jumped Varinia off in front and made the running while I lay handy in about sixth place.

'Down Tattenham Hill I moved up fourth. When I let Valoris go to the front 1½ furlongs from home, it was all over. We won on a tight rein by 2½ lengths from Berkeley Springs with Varinia three lengths away.

'When the dust of that row with Noel settled, I was so glad that I had turned freelance and, apart from Noel's reaction, I have never regretted it since. Of course I would have ridden Royal Palace and some other good ones, but I would never have been associated with horses like Sir Ivor and Nijinsky.

'Noel and I patched up our differences and I rode a winner for him at Newmarket on 13 July. I saw him through till the end of that season, when he engaged George Moore for the following year. He is a wonderful man, a great friend and was a magnificent trainer.

'Some jockeys prefer the retainer system. They know exactly where they are. Riding freelance is the breath of life to me. Which is why suspension is probably worse for me than for anyone else.'

Incidentally, after the race Varinia's owner, Marcus Wickham-Boynton said: 'My filly ran much better than we expected.' So it would surely have been most unfair to have made Lester ride her.

Nijinsky, of course, went back to the United States as soon as he had finished racing. It is a pity that we should be used in this manner. The Americans enjoy the benefit of having their horses trained by the best men in the world on our wonderful turf gallops and raced in our European prestige races for our top prize-money. Then, having acquired the status of a top international stallion worth upwards of two million pounds, they take the horse back to the United States. If it had stayed at home in the first place, it would probably have been broken down on the concrete-based dirt tracks. Thank heaven for the few men like Jim Joel, John Hislop and Michael Sobell who breed on the best lines and keep their great horses in the country.

I feel that any horse which is trained and raced in Europe for more than a year should be made to stand here as a stallion for at least three seasons and that this should be a condition of entry. Otherwise our classics lose all their value as the supreme racecourse tests, which establish the stallions of the future.

Lester has matured amazingly in the last few years. He is still a danger-man, always *sur un coup*, and I've no doubt that he will remain so. This is his magnetism. This is what makes him box-office so that sooner or later the racecourses will surely be paying him appearance money, as they do with the stars of motor-racing. But when he and Susan are at home in Newmarket with their two daughters, Maureen and Tracy, he will talk about racing's difficulties.

'Suspension is specially frustrating for me,' he says. 'It's a real punishment. Mind, I believe it's the only one that has any real effect on jockeys and, as such, I'm all for it. Fines mean very little. They are deducted from your account at Weatherby's and you don't notice them at all.

'Now suspensions are the accepted thing. A good thing too. The boys are all riding much better. I'm very glad that the Jockey Club are trying to have the same rules as other countries. But they must be enforced in the same way as in France and the United States. You can't have one set of rules or interpretation of the rules in one country and another somewhere else.'

He adds: 'The stewards must be consistent. This is one argument in favour of professional stewards. Otherwise we're all right as we are.'

He was, of course, born to jumping and had ridden schooling all his life. So, when he took out a National Hunt Licence it all came naturally. 'I enjoyed riding over hurdles very much. It was easy for me. You've got more time to think in a race.'

On trainers: 'Vincent O'Brien is a great trainer. So are Noel Murless and Paddy Prendergast.' Lester has already planned his training establishment in Newmarket. 'There are far too many good horses in Lambourn for the gallops. I wouldn't go back,' he says.

On non-triers: 'A lot of rubbish is talked about non-triers. Racing's straighter now than it's ever been. Most trainers today have to run a horse to get him fit. Many's the time I've ridden a two-year-old for Noel Murless and it hasn't known anything. You do your damndest and get as close as you can, but you're well beaten. Then next time it goes and wins a good race at Ascot and everyone says it wasn't trying the time before. Nowadays only a very few trainers can get a horse ready to win first time out.'

I was always brought up by Atty Persse to believe that that was the meaning of the word 'trainer' — a man who could train his horses at home so that they absolutely knew their jobs when they appeared in public.

Lester is tall for a jockey at 5 feet 7½ inches. 'There's an advantage in being tall. A horse responds to good weight on its back — live weight — not the dead weight of lead under the saddle to make up the right scale. On the whole I think the horse feels the authority of a big jockey. If you have a good length of leg, you can communicate more with the horse, squeeze him with your knees, control him generally — show him you are there.'

He admits, of course, that there are notable exceptions like the great American jockey Shoemaker, a genuine light-weight at little more than seven stone, and Sir Gordon Richards at eight stone.

Then there are the disadvantages of earning your living in a strenuous sport working about 1½ stone below your natural weight. 'Some people exaggerate how I live,' he says. 'I don't starve and I don't live on cigars and the *Financial Times*. And I don't drive to every race meeting in a rubber suit.'

But obviously he can't eat and drink what comes naturally to him.

'If I'm riding at eight stone six, I have a boiled egg for breakfast. If I have to do eight stone five that day, I'll give up the egg. I have a sandwich in the jockeys' room after I've finished riding and I always have a meal at night. You lose the habit of eating. The less you have, the less you want.'

On his family: 'Susan's a great influence on me. She's almost like my manager. She's a trainer's daughter, of course. And the two girls influence me, my daughters Maureen and

Tracy. If I'm getting too serious about something, they come in and one of them's bound to say something to make me laugh.'

Lester thinks of other jockeys and small trainers:

'I think more money ought to go back into racing. A lot of money is involved in the sport — especially in betting. The prize-money here is nothing like it is in France. Over there it can be four or five times as much. It's the small trainer that's affected. It's harder than ever for him to stay in the game in this country. And he's the backbone of racing. Perhaps I'm prejudiced because I'm the small trainer's son.'

Completely dedicated as he is, Lester will surely make a great trainer, particularly since he will have Susan at his side to help him. He understands horses, just as he has always had the will to win, so he will inevitably have the almost fanatical will to be as great a trainer as he has been a jockey.

It's like the wasting business, which has taken its toll of so many other jockeys; Lester's absolute devotion to racing makes it easier for him to give up things and, of course, the steadier he keeps it up, the easier it is for him to live with it.

'It's the wanting to win that matters,' he says. 'The competition. It's competing more than winning. In keeping your weight down you're competing with yourself. After a time it becomes a habit and you're in a long competition with yourself, and you only keep winning if you're trying to win all the time.

'If I got on the scales one morning intending to be 8 st 4 lbs and found that I was 8 st 6 lbs, even if I wasn't being asked to ride at 8 st 4 lbs I'd want to get those two pounds off. You've got to get what you started out to do. Otherwise you start getting beaten. The others start to beat you when you start being beaten by yourself.'

In the seventies Lester was entering upon the final phase of his riding career. It need not have been so. Horsemen, like Michael Beary, 'Brusher' Herbert, Davy Jones, etc., could go on to sixty plus. Acrobats are getting past it at forty. And Lester still insisted on being an acrobat riding shorter and shorter until he was making a travesty of jockeyship.

He had the results behind him, however, and as the top-class rivals faded one by one from the British scene, so Lester, one of the only real characters left in the game — a man with a will of his own, who had always known where he was going — ruled the roost in and out of the weighing room.

With the departure of George Moore, one of the only real world-class rivals still here was the late Bill Williamson, the quiet Australian, who had already ridden Lester out of it twice in the Arc de Triomphe.

In the Two Thousand Guineas of 1972 'the long fellow' elected to ride Bill Marshall's Grey Mirage, who, in the hands of the trainer's inexperienced son, had trotted up in two Guineas Trials.

John Galbreath's American colt Roberto, trained by Vincent O'Brien, was ridden in the Newmarket mile classic by 'Weary Willie'. Undoubtedly no one could have ridden better than Bill and I doubt whether Lester would have got to within half a length of Bernard van Cutsem's High Top.

Nevertheless, when the Derby came around, the Australian star's chance of achieving his life's ambition was frustrated. Lester eventually got the ride on Roberto at Epsom. And, although he put up a tremendous performance to beat Ernie Johnson on Rheingold by a short head, it left a very nasty taste in the mouths of all who knew that Williamson would have done every bit as well.

That was Lester's sixth Derby winner. He had equalled the all-time record set up by Jem Robinson and Steve Donoghue, although the latter's score included two war-time substitute Derbys on Pommern in 1915 and Gay Crusader in 1917.

The seventh so nearly came in the following year when Lester partnered Captain Marcos Lemos's Cavo Doro, a Sir Ivor colt with whom he had long been associated. The strong bay colt, earlier trained by Sam Armstrong, but now with Vincent O'Brien, looked the winner at the distance, but hung left under Lester's hard riding and was unable to get past Arthur Budgett's home-bred Morston who won by half a length in the hands of Edward Hide.

Despite this failure 1973 was a satisfying year. There were few peaks left to climb for Piggott, but the Arc de Triomphe had still eluded him. Fate was kind. Barry Hills had performed wonders with the previous year's Derby runner-up, Rheingold. Ridden by Yves Saint-Martin, the fine big bay had won four top races in the first half of the season: the John Porter Stakes at Newbury, the Prix Ganay at Longchamp, the Hardwicke Stakes at Royal Ascot and the Grand Prix de Saint-Cloud. Although beaten by Dahlia in the King George

VI and Queen Elizabeth Stakes at Ascot in July, it was clear that Rheingold would have a great chance in the Arc de Triomphe. However, in that race Saint-Martin would be claimed for the certain favourite, Daniel Wildenstein's brilliant filly, Allez France. So Lester stepped into his French rival's shoes and took over Barry Hills' four-year-old in the Benson and Hedges Gold Cup at York. He was beaten into third place, but Barry was not discouraged. At Longchamp in October, Rheingold looked magnificent, hard-trained and really well in himself. Lester had learnt the hard way from Williamson and Saint-Martin. Now he kept his mount in close touch with the leaders from the start and, taking the lead after entering the straight, rode on to a most impressive two-lengths victory over Allez France. That bogey had been laid.

Two years later Lester won both the Oaks and the Irish Guinness Oaks on the grand little Blakeney filly Juliette Marny, trained by Jeremy Tree at Beckhampton. In 1976 the Derby record was shattered.

The swarthy, French-based Egyptian Maurice Zilber picked the right man when he chose Lester for his deep-bodied, American-bred bay Vaguely Noble colt, Empery, owned by Bunker Hunt. This half-brother to the French One Thousand Guineas winner, Pampered Miss, and to two stakes winners in America had finished fourth in the French Guineas and third behind his stable-companion Youth in the Prix Lupin. At Epsom he was always holding a good position and came through under pressure to challenge inside the last quarter of a mile. Up the hill he went away comfortably and beat Relkino by three lengths. That was number seven and the record.

Twelve months later the Epsom specialist was back in that same coveted winner's circle again — this time on another colt trained by Vincent O'Brien.

Two years earlier, Vernons' Pools boss Robert Sangster and Vincent, helped at the time by a few partners, embarked on a bold policy which was to shake the entire racing world. Fed-up with buying other people's horses for their Coolmore/Castle Hyde set-up in Ireland, they decided to buy the best yearlings offered for sale at public auction at the top blood-stock sales in the northern hemisphere, race them and thus make their own stallions.

It was a policy that was to pay fantastic dividends besides giving European race-goers the privilege of watching the finest Thoroughbreds in the world in action.

That first crop included The Minstrel, Artaius, Be My Guest and Alleged. By the end of 1976 The Minstrel, a 200,000 dollar yearling by Northern Dancer, whose dam was half-sister to Nijinsky (also by Northern Dancer) had earned himself the highest rating in the British Isles after carrying Lester to an impressive victory in Newmarket's Dewhurst Stakes.

This chestnut colt with a predominance of white about him, who was to give the lie to many long-held superstitions, was unbeaten in three outings and was a worthy favourite for the following season's classic races.

After seeing the Sangster colt finish third to Nebbiolo in the Two Thousand Guineas at Newmarket and beaten a short head by Pampapaul in the Irish Two Thousand Guineas at The Curragh, I began to wonder whether *Anno Domini* was not finally catching up with 'the wonder-boy', whether he had not gone over the top at last. There is no doubt in my opinion that he did not excel in either contest.

As Robert Sangster and Vincent O'Brien, both bitterly disappointed, were leaving The Curragh racecourse, an official approached them and asked whether they would come back to the weighing-room where Piggott wished to talk to them.

Says Robert: 'There was half a bottle of champagne left from the earlier celebrations in the jockeys' changing-room. Vincent, Lester and I drank it out of china mugs. Lester told us that in his opinion The Minstrel was the best horse at that stage in Vincent's stable at Ballydoyle and that he would like to ride him in the Derby.

'We told him that if he would give his assurance that he would indeed partner the colt at Epsom, we would run him. He did so and the decision was made there and then.'

In that Derby Lester recovered all his old brilliance, and pulling out all the stops, drove The Minstrel up the hill to win by a neck from Hotgrove.

The colt was now improving remarkably. He went on to win the Irish Sweeps Derby at The Curragh and followed up with a magnificent victory in the King George VI and Queen Elizabeth Diamond Stakes at Ascot. Although slowly out of the stalls on the last occasion, he won a tremendous battle to beat Orange Bay by a short head.

The Canadian colt returned across the Atlantic with a syndicated price-tag on his head of over six million pounds. Artaius and Be My Guest, also showing a substantial profit, remained in Ireland for their stud careers. The Sangster policy was paying off with a vengeance. And there was still Alleged to come.

This handsome bay colt by Hoist the Flag won five of his six starts that season. His only defeat was certainly no disgrace. He just failed to stay Doncaster's 1¾ miles in the St Leger and was beaten 1½ lengths by the Queen's Dunfermline, finishing ten lengths clear of the third, Classic Example.

A few weeks later he proved himself the best horse in Europe when winning the 26-runner Prix de l'Arc de Triomphe at Longchamp. Lester sent him into the lead after nearly half a mile. Alleged quickened round the home turn and, as his jockey remembered the lessons of the past, opened up a four-length lead entering the straight and ran on strongly to hold off fast-finishing Balmerino by 1½ lengths.

The following year Alleged emulated the mighty Ribot, winning the Arc for the second successive year and carrying Lester to his third victory in the great European championship. That was the end of Alleged's magnificent career. He too, syndicated for about seven million pounds, returned across the Atlantic. Sangster's policy was showing the right return.

'We have been multiplying our outlay four times every season since we started,' says Robert. 'I'm not worried about the prize-money. That doesn't really count. It is the making of stallions and the value of those animals as stallions which justifies the whole operation.'

He added: 'Every year the only way you can balance how successful we are is by saying "they've bought thirty yearlings in 1977, thirty-three in 1978, twenty-seven in 1979 — what do they sell them for?" We're selling them well all the time. We're on a different key to the man who wants to race for fun. I'm afraid that he's paying too much for his yearlings. We're buying stallion pedigrees matched with looks and spreading the risk.'

Confirming that he and his partners quadruple their profits every year, Robert reckoned that anyone who could raise

£10 million to invest in bloodstock and £1½ million annual running costs could do the same as he; but for one single important factor. 'I have Vincent O'Brien,' he says. 'They have not. And there is only one Wizard of Tipperary.'

Owing to the virus, 1979 was a difficult season for Vincent O'Brien. But the two-year-olds were, according to Robert Sangster, the best that they had bought since the first crop, which included The Minstrel. When the Newmarket Houghton meeting came round, much depended on the performance of unbeaten Monteverdi.

'At last year's yearling sales we spent eight million dollars,' said Robert after his little chestnut colt had swept to victory. 'Now it's all justified. On the international market Monteverdi is already worth ten million dollars. This one horse has paid for the entire crop.'

All's well that ends well. But there could so easily have been disaster fifty yards from the post, when the brave little colt's head flew up, bringing a shout of dismay from the crowd.

Monteverdi, like his sire, Lyphard, is a small horse of the Hyperion type. With his comparatively short neck there is little in front of the saddle and Lester Piggott, riding with ludicrously short stirrup leathers, appeared likely to 'fall over the handlebars'.

Lester's whip was in his left hand and it seemed that, in a desperate effort to regain his balance, he inadvertently hit his mount's near cheek. When a young horse is doing his very best in only his fourth outing, such an act is enough to put him off for life.

Let me make one thing clear. A slap in the face is NOT part of the horseman's armoury. A true horseman never hits his horse on the head. In this case, the jockey's whip could so easily have flicked the colt's eye, discouraging him for life.

So the explanation that because Monteverdi was hanging so badly he wanted to teach him a lesson just does not hold water. The only lesson the colt could have learnt was NOT to try his best for fear of punishment. John Hislop, an outstanding rider and great judge, confirmed my own reading of the incident. 'He damn nearly fell off,' said John, of whom Sir Gordon Richards once said: 'Thank God he's not two stone lighter! He'd make us all go!'

We had seen the result of those ultra-short stirrup leathers at York, when Thatching was disqualified for swerving across the track. The jockey had no lateral control or impulsion from his legs. There have been other cases.

As a former trainer, for whom Lester, riding a normal length, rode a Newmarket winner at the age of fifteen, I am entitled to criticize. And, over the years, entirely alone, I have never ceased to do so in face of frequent hostility.

In the autumn of 1979 racing's superb monthly magazine *Pacemaker International* featured an Australian supplement, whose splendid illustrations revealed that all the top jockeys 'down under' ride at the normal classical length like Jimmy Lindley and his friend, champion Joe Mercer. They can use their legs to drive and guide.

It's a very sad thing about 45-year-old Lester, who has ridden so many incredible races in the past. Unless he lets his leathers down to an Australian length, he must retire now.

British racing — owners, breeders, trainers and even jockeys, who grotesquely imitate him, and, particularly the punting public — can no longer afford the luxury of pandering to Piggott.

The cover of an earlier edition of *Pacemaker*, a brilliant photographic study by Gerry Cranham, showed Piggott cantering down on Crimson Beau, riding so short that he can only remain there by hanging on for grim death to the horse's gaping mouth and, like a young apprentice, to his neckstrap. His seat is not independent enough to 'teach a horse a lesson' by playing around with his whip.

Lester should hang up his boots. They might even command a good price. So short does he ride that only the ankles can show many signs of wear!

Lester is not only one of the greatest jockeys the world has ever seen; he is also a remarkable man. Without doubt he is still one of the star figures in British sport and he is one of the few real characters left in racing. Like the motto on the horseboxes from his old home, Lambourn, Lester in his heyday was 'A distance in front of the others'.

Let's keep that memory.

2

Joe Mercer

At last he's the champion!

Throughout the Piggott period Joe Mercer has provided steady opposition to 'the long fellow'. Now in his forties, he is a first-class jockey and a credit to the racing scene.

A year older than his friend, Bradford-born Joe was still a half-a-crown-a-week apprentice with Major Fred Sneyd at Sparsholt when he rode his first winner three years after he had signed on.

The son of a coach painter, he was born on 25 October 1934. Although there was no racing blood in his family, Joe, while still at school, helped with the tack cleaning and mucking out at a local riding stable in return for the odd ride on a pony. In the meantime, his elder brother, Manny — later to be killed at Ascot — had joined George Colling at Newmarket and was doing as well as might be expected of one of the most brilliant natural young riders ever to grace the British turf.

So well, in fact, that Major Fred Sneyd, who had trained the brothers, Eph and Doug Smith, wrote to Mr Mercer asking: 'Are there any more at home like him?' Joe leapt at the chance and was sent to Sparsholt.

That was just before I went as assistant trainer to Atty Persse. Sneyd, like my guv'nor, kept his apprentices so short of pocket-money, that Joe was still earning only half-a-crown a week when he rode his first winner three years later.

Soon after, his wages rose to ten shillings a week and remained there until he finished his time in 1955 when he had ridden nearly two hundred winners, including the Oaks.

In the early stages he sometimes received even less money at the end of the week than the pittance he was allowed. All through his time he was fined sixpence every time he fell off.

In those days there was no question of any Sunday off. 'I

had one night off a week,' he said, 'and worked from 6 a.m. till 11 p.m. As well as riding out and working in the yard, I had to help in the house, I started off as kitchen boy and ended up waiting at table. I had to feed the dogs and cats, too.'

He added: 'Towards the end of my time, I lived with the family and was even allowed a glass of sherry before dinner. Major Sneyd was a good master and taught me well. Even though I naturally wanted to follow in Manny's footsteps, I don't think I ever tried to copy his style of riding. I always rode as I was taught by the Major.'

It was Ambiguity who gave Joe his big chance in the Oaks of 1953. He seized it with both hands. Tenth of the twenty-one runners entering the Epsom straight, the apprentice delivered a perfectly timed challenge to beat the Aga Khan's Kerkeb. Manny's mount, Happy Laughter, who had won the One Thousand Guineas, was fourth.

It is fair to say that Joe's whole career was made by this success. Ambiguity's trainer, Jack Colling, that most charming of men, who had just moved from Newmarket to West Ilsley, gave him a retainer.

The partnership prospered so well that when Jack retired in 1962, Joe signed up again with his successor, Dick Hern. The continuing association of trainer, jockey and the stable's owners, notably Jakey Astor, was one of the best features of British racing.

With his clear, concise brain, Joe, like most jockeys, prefers to ride a waiting race. But he is perfectly capable of of waiting in front, if these tactics are forced on him.

He is a classical English stylist, riding with a long rein and a sensible length of stirrup leather, which allows him the use of his legs to correct tired horses and keep them perfectly balanced when they start to roll about in heavy going. Moreover in a tight finish he can really sit down into a horse and get behind him to drive him home.

Loyalty, as the keystone of Joe's life, has paid immense dividends. When, in the summer of 1970, Sir Gordon Richards, finally forced to quit William Hill's Whitsbury Stables, announced that he would have to give up training, his chief owner, Michael Sobell, bought the West Ilsley stables from Jakey Astor. He hoped that Gordon, who had just taken on Edward Hide as stable-jockey as the successor to Scobie Breasley, would be able to continue training for him and Lady Beaverbrook in the famous yard.

Jakey, however, had other ideas. In what must have been one of the strangest deals he sold his training establishment only on condition that Dick Hern remained as trainer and Joe as jockey.

Since that Ambiguity year of 1953, when he finished with sixty-one winners, Joe has remained firmly, but always quietly, among the leading riders.

In February 1959 he married Anne, daughter of the Royal Jockey, Harry Carr, who had already made a name for herself as a horsewoman. She had won more than fifty first prizes, collected more than two hundred rosettes in the show-ring and finished fourth in the hack class at the Royal International Show at the White City in 1956.

A year before his marriage, Joe broke his neck riding in Singapore. Another year, a broken arm prevented him from winning all five classic races in Bombay. At the time when he was injured, he had already won the Two Thousand and One Thousand Guineas. His father-in-law came out to substitute and win the Derby and the Leger on the horses he would have ridden. 'He'd have won the Oaks too, if he'd known his filly as well as I did,' says Joe.

Occasional injuries of varying severity are the lot of every professional horseman, but in June 1972 Joe emerged as a national hero after a truly horrible accident. The light aircraft which was taking him to the races crashed during take-off from Newbury. Although badly shaken, Joe escaped injury and, with complete disregard for the imminent and almost inevitable explosion, pulled his fellow passengers, including leading trainer Bill Marshall, out of danger. He had barely got them clear when the plane burst into flames. The pilot, unhappily, had died in the crash.

The next day Joe was a front-page hero in every newspaper. But the racing world wondered whether he would be fit for Brigadier Gerard in Royal Ascot's Prince of Wales' Stakes. This was the one ride which he could not give up. He performed with such supreme confidence that John Hislop's great colt, inspired by the rider he knew so well, trounced his field and flew home to win like a true champion in record time.

Until 1970 Joe had always held firm to the belief that

Hornbeam was the best horse he had ever ridden. That gallant little chestnut colt had won eleven races from a mile to two miles, including the Great Voltigeur Stakes. He failed by half a length to give 23 lbs to Morcambe in the Ebor and was beaten a whisker by French Beige in the Doncaster Cup. Although he did not win a classic, Hornbeam finished only three-quarters of a length behind Cambremer in the 1956 St Leger.

I shall always remember Doncaster. I was training at the time and enjoying a most successful season with my small string at Upper Lambourn. I had always admired Jack Colling, who was particularly kind and helpful to young trainers like myself, and envied his beautifully-run Yorkshire grouse moor. I asked him how the birds were and whether the prospects were good. He said: 'It's a splendid season, but it's properly messed up. For the first time for years I've got to go to Doncaster. I have this runner in the Leger and my owners think I ought to go and saddle him and see him run. Certainly he must have a bit of a chance, but I think it's most unreasonable!'

The Mercers' attractive house just outside Newbury, overlooking the River Kennet, is called 'Hornbeam'. But in 1970 another horse appeared — a handsome bay colt by Queen's Hussar, bred, owned and broken by leading racing journalist John Hislop, the best amateur rider on the flat I have ever seen or am likely to see, in partnership with his equally enthusiastic wife, Jean.

Good horses deserve good names. You seldom find a decent animal with a bad one. Passifyoucan was always being passed and Jack Olding's Winagain never won at all.

The Hislops' colt was by Queen's Hussar out of La Paiva by Prince Chevalier. They gave him the superb name of Conan Doyle's hero, Brigadier Gerard. How delighted that happily conceited French cavalry officer would have been to find his name carried by one of the greatest horses of the time. He would, of course, have considered it only right and proper!

Dick Hern and Joe handled the colt beautifully to win four races in his two-year-old season. But, partly because of his sire, who was not really expected to produce classic winners, he was generally believed to be outclassed by Mill Reef and David Robinson's unbeaten My Swallow, who disputed favouritism for the Two Thousand Guineas.

Badly drawn in the Prix Robert Papin at Maisons-Laffitte the previous year, Mill Reef's only defeat had been by a whisker at the hands of My Swallow, who had gone on to become the first English horse to win all the French two-year-old 'classics' and our highest-ever juvenile stakes winner.

This pair were considered so outstanding that the Guineas field in 1971 was the smallest since mighty Ormonde won for the Duke of Westminster in 1886. Both the cracks had won their first races of the new season, Mill Reef was now made favourite at 6 to 4 with his rival, easier in the market, at 2 to 1. Brigadier Gerard was next in demand at 11 to 2. As the six runners paraded, John Hislop said: 'I have a first-class trainer and jockey. They assure me that my horse is supremely fit and did not want a preliminary outing. That's good enough for me.'

So it proved. Frank Durr made the running on My Swallow until the Bushes where Joe sent Brigadier Gerard smoothly into the lead. Geoff Lewis on Mill Reef tried desperately to get on terms going down into the Dip and up the hill, but was still three lengths behind at the winning post with My Swallow three-quarters of a length away third.

As the year progressed Mill Reef continued on his classic way, embracing the Derby and culminating in the Arc de Triomphe. It was generally assumed that he had been defeated in the Guineas by a slightly inferior colt — a brilliant miler, trained specially for his only classic engagement, and that the Brigadier would never beat him again. This view was strengthened when the Hislop colt scraped home by a head from Sparkler in the St James's Palace Stakes on Royal Ascot's very soft going.

The going was soft at Goodwood, but the lovely old course drains better than Ascot and Joe won the Sussex Stakes with consummate ease, making all the running to beat the French challenge, Faraway Son, by five lengths.

At Ascot, in September, he beat another French horse, Dictus, by a contemptuous eight lengths in the Queen Elizabeth II Stakes as a curtain-raiser to his last race of the year, Newmarket's Champion Stakes, now boosted to £25,280. This was the Brigadier's first outing over a distance beyond a mile and those who doubted his stamina felt fully justified when, after taking the lead before the Bushes, he only just held off the challenge of Paddy Prendergast's 20 to

1 four-year-old Rarity by a short head to retain his unbeaten record. The doubters had ignored the fact that the Newmarket going was unusually soft on this last day of the Houghton meeting.

With typical courage the Hislops, who had turned down enormous offers for their horse, decided to keep him in training as a four-year-old but at the same time did not intend to run him again on soft ground.

'A good horse acts in any going' is a particularly stupid, trite saying. Many of the best horses have, like Brigadier Gerard, a lovely low sweeping action. How could you expect such a daisy-cutter to gallop through a ploughed field? Equally the horse with a high action, usually associated with stayers, brings his feet down hard and is totally unsuited to firm ground, although he revels in the soft. It is purely mathematical.

1972 was to be the great year. First the Brigadier won the 1 mile Lockinge Stakes on his home course, Newbury. Then, reverting to one mile and a quarter, he won the Westbury Stakes at Sandown. At Royal Ascot, Joe was still very shaken by his aircraft crash, but was still determined to ride his wonder horse. Seldom have I seen more confidence. Travelling strongly on the bit from the start, he swept into the lead a quarter of a mile out and streaked home to win by five lengths from Steel Pulse, who was receiving 3 lbs more than weight for age and was shortly to endorse the form by winning the Irish Sweeps Derby. Joe could scarcely hear the tumultuous cheers. Delayed shock had set in and he collapsed as he was unsaddling.

So to Sandown and the Eclipse, which had been hailed as the 'Race of the Century', as it was expected to produce a clash with Mill Reef. Unhappily the little American champion had become a victim of the virus which crippled racing during this season.

Heavy rain had softened Sandown's famous Eclipse course, which is stiff enough at the best of times, and the Hislops were tempted to withdraw. But the opposition appeared so weak that they decided to let their colt take his chance. He started at 11 to 4 on and beat Gold Rod by a length, obviously hating the going but typically never giving in. John Hislop declared: 'We will never again run him on soft ground.'

In common with most great horses the Brigadier is lazy.

Sometimes Joe had to ride like a demon to counteract the bone idleness of a colt who knew exactly how much was needed to win and wouldn't do a damn thing more. But never once was there the slightest sign of his being ready to quit near the finish. Always that handsome head was thrust out, battling on and on as if there were no limit.

His temperament was so wonderful that when, still unbeaten after fourteen starts, he was saddled for the £60,202 King George VI and Queen Elizabeth Stakes at Ascot, now sponsored by the diamond people, De Beers, his connections made no secret of their confidence in his ability to stay 1½ miles in top-class company.

There was the Italian Derby winner, Gay Lussac, ridden by Lester Piggott; Steel Pulse, fresh from his Irish triumph with Bill Williamson in the saddle again; Riverman (Freddie Head), winner of the French Guineas, and Parnell (Willie Carson), who had won the 1971 Irish St Leger. Jim Joel's Selhurst (Geoff Lewis), the half-brother to Royal Palace, was probably the best of the other four starters.

John Hislop told my colleague on the *Sun*, Claude Duval: 'I'm certain that no horse in the world could beat mine from one mile to one mile and a quarter on firm going — and that includes Mill Reef. But to be judged the best of all time, he must win at 1½ miles.

'Ribot was a middle-distance horse, and was bred with more stamina. But our horse has such a relaxed style that he does not take a lot out of himself, and I think he'll stay on. At four years old, he's at his peak.

'Owning him is a fairy tale come true. As a journalist I used to write about Ribot's wins. But I never dreamed that one day I'd breed and own a horse who could be mentioned in the same breath as Ribot.

'If he wins tomorrow I'm told that he will top £200,000 in prize money, but I honestly couldn't tell you how much he's won. I'm not interested in that aspect of racing. Last year we could have won a lot more money by hawking him around France. But he wouldn't be half the horse now.

'It's still difficult for me and my wife, Jean, to believe we actually own this colt. I used to win races on hunter chasers, a far cry from the Brigadier, for whom we turned down an offer of £250,000 as a two-year-old.

'Now in the form books he is rated higher than Nijinsky,

who went to stud for two million. People approach me with blank cheques, and he's so valuable that I can't even insure him for anything like his true value.

'But I will never sell him and, at the end of the season, he'll go back to the Egerton Stud at Newmarket where he was foaled.

'The only thing he hates is rain. He has such fine skin, and I hope that the weather continues dry, and the going is like a brick at Ascot. His only gimmick is that he likes to go into the horsebox backwards. This was printed in an article recently, but after the Eclipse, he walked straight into his box headfirst. So, he's obviously been reading the papers.

'I hope he's about fourth or fifth into the straight tomorrow, and that there is not a crawl, or a mad pace. Then, at the turn, if I was riding him, I'd make the best way home.

'Yves Saint-Martin says that Riverman is the best French horse for ten years, and I suppose the Italian, Gay Lussac, could be another Ribot.

'If the Brigadier does win it will only be two or three days afterwards that it occurs to us that we have picked up another £60,000.'

Sir Gordon Richards, too, talked to Claude before the race. Twenty-six times champion and winner of 4,870 races, he said:

'Brigadier Gerard is one of the finest horses of all time. His unbeaten record as a two-, three-, and four-year-old proves this. He's got such guts that he just won't be beaten.

'For a horse to be called great, he must be unbeaten. That's why Ribot and Bahram were so outstanding. But, if Brigadier Gerard does win the King George, we must certainly put him in this bracket.

'Unbeaten horses fascinate me. We never really know just how great they are. I believe Brigadier Gerard will get 1½ miles for the first time. He's got such a wonderful temperament.

'Before Ribot won the same race in 1956 another horse bolted and delayed the start. But Ribot just stood there on three legs, and couldn't have cared less.

'Then the race started and he made mincemeat of his rivals. That was greatness. You can see the same qualities in the Brigadier.'

When they jumped out of the stalls, Geoff Lewis made the

running on Selhurst. Before the six-furlong marker, however, Willie Carson had sent Parnell into the lead and it was obvious that the Brigadier's stamina was going to be thoroughly tested.

Joe, who had once again been riding with supreme confidence, made a forward move in Swinley Bottom and was second entering the straight, where he soon ranged upsides with Parnell. One and a half furlongs from home he hit the front and the cheering started, only to diminish with fear as the favourite crossed over his rivals towards the far rails.

Forced to switch to the outside, Parnell was starting to come again, but the winning post arrived too soon and he was beaten by 1½ lengths with Riverman 5 lengths away third and Steel Pulse fourth. The Italian challenge was fifth nearly ten lengths behind the Brigadier.

A steward's inquiry inevitably followed. After seeing the film they exonerated Brigadier Gerard and we were all delighted with the verdict as the Queen presented diamond trinkets to the Hislops, Dick Hern and Joe.

Nevertheless, the finish highlighted yet again the discrepancy in the interpretation of the rules between our amateur stewards on different racecourses in England and, particularly, their professional counterparts in other countries, which has frequently caused trouble for our jockeys abroad. There is no doubt that the Brigadier would have won in any case. But if this is to be taken into account when a rule is broken, it should be clearly stated. Otherwise the letter of the law must be obeyed and the winner might well have lost the race in France, Australia or the United States. Parnell's trainer, Bernard van Cutsem, summed up: 'Brigadier Gerard was certainly the better horse on this going. But he definitely took our ground.' It was a happy ending and a wonderful day for British breeding.

Richard Baerlein, as fine a turf writer as the Brigadier's owner — and that means the best of all time — wrote:

'Everything connected with the Brigadier is pleasing to every section of the racing community. It is the finest example ever known in history of how to handle a thoroughbred racehorse to the best of his advantage.

'Not until his fifteenth race was he first tested for stamina at 1½ miles. By then he was fully matured in every respect and has mastered the 1¼ mile races, which at one stage were even in doubt. After the Guineas he was considered a miler.

'Some horses stay a mile as a two-year-old and only seven furlongs later in life. Many people backed Stintino for the Derby two years ago because he won over 1¼ miles as a two-year-old. He only stayed about 100 yards further as a three-year-old. I believe the Brigadier stays 1¼ miles this year far better than he did last.'

Richard notes: 'Tom Watson, who compiles a private handicap for the benefit of *Raceform* subscribers and readers of *The Racehorse*, says his figures make the Brigadier the best horse he has ever rated. He has many years' experience of handicapping horses and I find his figures more compelling than wordy arguments.'

Tom goes on: 'If we allow Steel Pulse to have run to his Irish Sweeps Derby mark and Parnell to my rating of his win in the Rouge Dragon Handicap at Ascot in April, the mark the Brigadier returned on Saturday was just 4 lbs below the best mark I have for him over his ideal distance of 1¼ miles!'

John Oaksey, that other turf writer so eminently deserving to be bracketed with Hislop and Baerlein wrote: 'No horse in the history of the turf has been better, more openly or more boldly managed than this one and, as far as I am concerned, if the Brigadier retired tomorrow, he would still have done more — very much more — than enough.'

John noted: 'Before the race, knowing Brigadier Gerard's tendency to idle, Dick Hern had told Joe Mercer not to be afraid of giving him a slap if it was needed. But it never was and, striding powerfully home, the Brigadier showed not the slightest sign of weariness, fatigue or lack of stamina. The bogey of those two extra furlongs was well and truly laid.'

A great deal of the credit must go to Joe. In the lower echelons it is the trainer and his lads who make the horse. The flat-race jockey, riding like a monkey up a stick, has little or no influence on the production of the youngster as an effective racing machine, capable of earning money for its owner. Only those horsemen, who have ridden and trained jumpers, can appreciate the enormous help which an experienced jockey can give to a novice horse. Put Jonjo O'Neill up first time out, ride your horse again afterwards and see what I mean. It's a different animal. The same applies to the production of a top-class flat horse. And there is no doubt that despite the skill and know-how of his owner and trainer,

Brigadier Gerard's greatness must owe a lot to the expert, sympathetic handling of his devoted rider.

A smart, well-dressed businessman with a controlling interest in two first-class garages already, Joe may not want to train. Why take on all that thankless worry when, after starting as a half-a-crown-a-week apprentice, you have deservedly 'got it made'? He has earned plenty of time to enjoy his favourite hobbies of shooting and fishing.

I believe that Joe has learnt and improved his riding more than any other jockey in recent years. They say that 'Life begins at forty!' Well, 1974 brought three classic successes which gave Joe immense pleasure.

Now that Dick Hern's stables housed a number of the Queen's horses, his jockey frequently wore the famous purple, scarlet, black and gold colours just as his father-in-law had done.

In marked contrast to the previous lean years since Canisbay had won the Eclipse in 1965, the Queen's horses won over half a million pounds in prize-money in the eight years following the appointment of Lord Porchester as her racing manager in 1969. For Her Majesty to have bred and owned the winners of four classic races in as many years was a magnificent triumph.

Highclere, a big, rich bay filly by Queen's Hussar out of Highlight, had a beautiful low action and was well suited by top of the ground conditions. She was so highly strung, however, that she could have become a 'real lady' but for the horse-sense of her trainer and the sympathetic handling of her 'lad', Betty Brister, at home, and of her jockey, Joe Mercer, on the gallops and on the racecourse.

Highclere soon showed Hern that she had undoubted ability. Nevertheless, her two-year-old form was, at first sight, somewhat disappointing. She ran three times — at Newmarket, Ascot and Newbury — finishing second on the first two occasions and, on her final outing, winning the second division of the Donnington Maiden Stakes unimpressively, staring about her during the race. At this stage neither Dick nor Joe was particularly happy about the Royal filly as a classic prospect. But no one knew her sire, Queen's Hussar, better than Henry Porchester. After all, the horse was owned by his father, Lord Carnarvon, and stood at their Highclere Stud near Newbury where the Sussex Stakes winner had already sired so many winners, including the outstanding classic performer Brigadier Gerard.

The Royal racing manager knew that Queen's Hussar had run his best races when equipped with blinkers by his trainer, the late Atty Corbett. Happily Porchester is that all-too-rare commodity: a modern owner who really understands horses and racing from A to Z. Make no mistake; the Queen would not have chosen him otherwise.

The typical modern owner on this side of the Atlantic strongly resents the innocent suggestions that his horse should run in blinkers next time out. If he does, the trainer knows that he will win. The animal is, let us suppose, very fit but in his last two races he has been looking about him, not paying attention to the job in hand. You would do the same if you were a big horse being impelled solely by a little man riding with ultra-short stirrup leathers, scrubbing about on top like a chimp on an elephant. The horse may be as honest as the day is long, but all he needs is blinkers to keep his mind on the job.

Our grandfathers, born in the happy years before cars appeared, had to rely on the horse for everything: to do their shopping; to travel around, or to get the doctor for a sick child. Inevitably they had to know more about the animal than we usually do today in this highly mechanized age. So often their ideas were based on plain commonsense and considerably kinder than methods employed now.

At the turn of the century, the American jockey Tod Sloan's influence began to be felt, and all riders started to adopt short stirrup leathers like 'a monkey up a stick', as it was then described. The trainers had to find some other means of impulsion. The power of the driving legs had been diminished and excessive use of the whip would only sour the horse off.

So, whenever necessary, they fitted blinkers. They knew their value. After all, every cart and carriage horse had to be equipped with blinkers (or winkers) to stop him shying at things in the hedge, to keep his mind on the job and to make him provide safe conveyance. They were normal, necessary and required by law as the side-lights on a car are today.

It was no reflection on the horse's honesty. Some of the most genuine animals in turf history have been useless without them; these include Felicitation, Alycidon, National

Spirit, Durante — one of the best and bravest handicappers of our time — and his sister, Royal Hunt Cup winner, Val d'Assa. The last two were among the many fine horses that Atty Persse trained in the final years of his long and glorious career while I was his assistant trainer. Nearly all our three- and four-year-old colts wore blinkers. The late Lord Sefton's flying Nasrullah filly Nassau was never without them, even at exercise, after she had whipped round at the start when heavily fancied first time out at Kempton. Nothing daunted, Atty fitted blinkers next time. He, Sefton and Jack Olding doubled their bet next time out and she flew in. Nassau won six of her twelve starts that season, but from that moment she never even left her box without her black hat. Blinkers were additionally useful in her case. They stopped her looking behind her and thus selecting targets to kick. She could go backwards almost as fast as she could go forwards to deliver a well-aimed *coup de pied*. We had a court-case when, free from her blinkers so that the jockey could weigh in after the Queen Mary Stakes at Ascot, she kicked a woman and broke her jaw. But in a race she was as game a battler as you would ever find and, if her owner had not insisted on having her home and turning her out at Crocksteth during the winter, she would, according to her trainer, have won the One Thousand Guineas instead of finishing fourth.

Unhappily, between the World Wars, a racing journalist described blinkers as 'the rogue's mask'. The phrase stuck and was used again and again. I hope that ignorant fellow turns uncomfortably in his grave every time a trainer is discouraged from fitting blinkers and a horse suffers an unnecessary hiding. I once asked Atty how much blinkers improved Durante, winner of two Jubilees. 'At least two stone,' he replied.

Now Joe rides a much more sensible length than most of today's jockeys, sadly influenced as they are by the example of Lester Piggott. But even Joe rides very short. Moreover, you don't want too much leg with a temperamental filly like Highclere. Porchester knew much more about racehorses than Sefton. The Queen readily agreed with his suggestion that, after her Newbury victory in September, Highclere should go back for a rest to the Highclere Stud. But there was no question of her staying there over Christmas. In November, looking supremely well and relaxed, she returned to Hern's stables at West Ilsley to keep warm through the winter months.

During the winter, while Highclere was trotting on the roads right through until the end of January, she was the subject of several fruitful discussions. Porchester, a stickler for detail, had noticed that the times of Highclere's races were fast. Moreover, Polygamy was very highly rated by Peter Walwyn. In Highclere's first race, in the July Stakes at Newmarket, she had been beaten by Louis Freedman's game little bay who had had the benefit of a previous outing. Next time out, although second again, Highclere turned the tables on Polygamy.

Porchester believes in drawing up a plan of campaign, which, if then approved by the Queen, is put into action. Highclere started cantering in February when the weather came right. Although doing really well, she was still backward in her coat and it was decided to run her first time out in the One Thousand Guineas wearing blinkers. They undoubtedly helped her to concentrate and the surprise factor of blinkers first time in public had to be taken into consideration. Joe rode her in home-work and in a gallop on Newbury race-course. Henry Porchester and Dick Hern went to Newmarket with high hopes. The bold policy succeeded admirably. Joe rode a blinder in the classic. Always laying up on the pace, he kicked on from the Bushes, trying to establish as great a lead as possible going down into the Dip. Pat Eddery and Poly-gamy joined battle up the final hill and a ding-dong struggle ensued right to the line. Joe said: 'My mare just stuck her head out and would not give in.' But neither jockey was certain of the result as they rode in. A great cheer went up when the result was announced. The photo-finish camera showed that the Queen's filly had just held on to win by inches. It was the second home-bred classic winner for Her Majesty, who had won the Two Thousand Guineas with Pall Mall over the same course in 1958.

After the race another bold move was decided upon in the winner's enclosure when the Queen herself reasoned that such a long-striding filly would not be suited to the sharp Epsom circuit and decided that instead Highclere should go to Chantilly for the Prix de Diane (French Oaks).

It was a decision which was to provide all Highclere's connections and the racing world in general with an unforgettable experience. Fortune favours the brave and there is no doubt about the courage behind that June venture in 1974. Naturally there were doubts about whether highly-strung Highclere would travel well by air. They were soon to be allayed. She flew happily from Southampton to Le Bourget and was in fine, ferocious fettle to greet her people on that sunny Sunday morning two days later.

With the Queen travelled Lord and Lady Porchester and the Royal Stud Manager, Michael Oswald. The French crowds were as thrilled by our Queen's visit as they had been when she had visited the Normandy studs. They lined the route shouting 'Vive la Reine! Vive la Reine Elizabeth! Vive la Duchesse!' (The last greeting was puzzling until it was realized that the dukedom of Normandy was traditionally one of the subsidiary titles of the British monarch.) Dick Hern, Joe Mercer and their wives, Sheilah and Anne, flew to Le Bourget from Newbury on the morning of the race.

Despite its small, antiquated stands, which contrast vividly with the superlative glorious tribunes of Longchamp, Chantilly is one of the world's finest and loveliest racecourses. As a backdrop it has the magnificent château and the Grande Ecurie (the Great Stables) which is as large as a palace. The track itself is not dissimilar to The Curragh, although the bends at the bottom end are sharper. It comprises a long back stretch down to the stables turn and then two fairly sharp right-handed bends and a home straight of just under half a mile on the collar to the winning post.

Chantilly is, of course, the Newmarket of France. With Lamorlaye, the neighbouring village, it combines to make by far the biggest training centre in the country. Les Aigles have some of the finest all-weather gallops anywhere and the famous historic forest, noted for its hunting, is interlaced with sand rides. The atmosphere is distinctly 'Franglais'. Racing universally can never escape from English, the language of its origin. In the town itself there are constant reminders. There is the Relais du Jockey Club and the Cafe Tipperary, whose omelette, even in that land of gourmets, is renowned as a culinary masterpiece.

Having lunched, the Herns and the Mercers were already on the course to greet the Queen when she arrived, driving down the track in an open car in an atmosphere of great Gallic excitement.

Really good jockeys always talk to the stable-lads. Joe Mercer belongs to that rare breed and he knows the value of discussing their charges with the dedicated lads and lasses who spend their time with them. Highclere was quiet and off-colour only when she was coming in season. Betty Brister was able to reassure the jockey that the filly was in tremendous high-spirited form. She needed to be because she had twenty-one opponents in the classic including her stable-companion Gaily, who had won the Irish One Thousand Guineas.

The Prix de Diane is run over one mile and two and a half furlongs and the Chantilly going was fast — ideal for Highclere. The favourite was Jack Cunnington's Comtesse de Loir. Bunker Hunt's Hippodamia was also strongly fancied.

Once again Joe rode the sort of inspired professional race we have come to expect of him in any country and in any circumstances. From the jump-off they went a good gallop and as they turned into the long home straight he had the blinkered Highclere in third place behind Hippodamia. Two furlongs out that filly drifted away from the rails. Joe seized his opportunity, picked up the Royal filly, shot through the gap and went right away to win by two lengths from Comtesse de Loir.

Fantastic scenes greeted the Royal triumph. It was the first time ever that any filly had won both the One Thousand Guineas and the Prix de Diane.

As the Herns and Mercers flew back after accomplishing this wonderful feat, they received a radio message inviting them to dinner with the Royal Family at Windsor Castle. Joe said later: 'It was the greatest day of our lives.' And this sentiment was echoed by Lord Porchester.

The Racing Manager's honorary post requires a great deal of travelling, which he enjoys. He is particularly keen to watch all the Queen's two-year-olds first time out, and is always present when there is a runner in a sponsored race.

Porchester is an immense admirer of the Queen's knowledge of racing, her ability to read a race and her judgment of the make and shape of a racehorse — not forgetting the very great knowledge of pedigrees which Her Majesty has amassed over the years.

His ambition is to help the Queen to breed and race the winner of the Derby, and all his efforts and those of the team of trainers, Stud Manager and staff are geared to achieve that ambition. As we will see when we write about Willie Carson, Dunfermline has proved this.

After twenty-five years as first jockey at West Ilsley, first under Jack Colling and then under Dick Hern, Joe was succeeded by Willie at the end of the 1976 season.

Fate moves in a mysterious way. This was the time when Sir Noel Murless retired and handed over wonderful Warren Place, Newmarket, to his son-in-law, Henry Cecil, who had already won the Two Thousand Guineas twice and was aiming for a permanent place as Britain's leading trainer.

Henry needed a top retained jockey. There was one available. He signed up Joe and, not surprisingly, the partnership has flourished. I don't think that even Joe appreciated the significance of the move at that time.

His new employer is in the direct line of succession not only to his father-in-law, in my opinion our greatest flat trainer, but also to Sir Noel's predecessor, the little martinet of Beckhampton, Fred Darling.

Since the First World War it was the retainer which carried with it the Jockeys' Championship. Steve Donoghue, Sir Gordon Richards (25 times), Lester Piggott . . . .

By the start of the 1979 season Joe was firmly established as stable-jockey to Warren Place. The writing was on the wall early when he and Henry nearly pulled off the Newmarket classic double achieved by Noel in 1967 with Fleet and Royal Palace.

First they landed the One Thousand Guineas with One in a Million. In the Two Thousand Guineas on Saturday Joe rode the stable's unbeaten favourite, Kris, owned by Jockey Club Senior Steward, Lord Howard de Walden.

A typically polished Mercer performance saw Kris mastering his rivals and looking all over a winner in the lead a furlong out only to be overhauled up the famous hill by a brilliantly-timed, desperate, last-second flourish from young American star Steve Cauthen on 20 to 1 outsider Tap On Wood.

Thereafter Joe and the magnificent chestnut Kris, who seemed to improve with every race, were never again beaten that season and the colt was hailed as Europe's champion miler. It was a great pity, however, that Tap On Wood's sickness prevented another meeting between these two grand horses.

As the season went on, Henry's score rose to a new high and, despite the successes of all-conquering Troy, he passed the prize-money total of Dick Hern to beat his own records in both winners and cash.

Suddenly, inevitably, Joe found himself opening up the gap between himself and Willie Carson, the holder of his old job with Hern. Suddenly he was champion at the age of 45 — the genuine, deserving British Champion Jockey of 1979.

As long as Henry Cecil's supremacy continues and unless there is an irresistible challenge from Steve Cauthen, John Reid or . . . dare I suggest, Bill Shoemaker, Joe is likely to stay on top until he retires.

I salute the champion!

3

Edward Hide

Edward Hide rode Forbear for me at Chester. He was only a boy, apprenticed to his father, Shropshire farmer Bill, one of the nicest men ever to hold a trainer's licence. She was a bonny, dark bay two-year-old filly, full of potential — the epitome of that old-time recipe, 'the head of an angel and the backside of a cook'. But she was still as buxom as a barmaid — she had been very well done at the Lambourn Stud — and I couldn't get the weight off at home. So she needed the race, but it was important that she should not be hurt.

I thought the sharp track would suit her and I gave Edward the only orders that it is fair to give to a boy, as I had been taught by Atty Persse: 'Get as close as you can, but don't knock her about'.

I didn't know my jockey, though he was already being hailed as a most promising young rider. I did know that, if he even touched my filly with the whip, I'd crucify him.

He rode her quite beautifully, kept her balanced throughout and gave her every chance. She finished close-up fifth and I was absolutely delighted. She had had a perfect education that would stand her in good stead for the rest of her days.

A week later Edward came up to me at another meeting. 'Did that filly eat up all right, sir?' he asked. In that moment I knew that any boy as dedicated to his horses as this just had to be a great jockey.

Charlie Elsey, who will always remain my 'beau ideal' of a trainer, thought so too and lost no time in signing him up. 'That lad knows everything that goes on in every race,' he told me. 'If I were a betting man I could make a fortune on the things he tells me. He's a fine jockey and, at the same time, a great help to his trainer.'

Edward rode 131 winners in 1957 and topped the century

again in the following two seasons. He finished third on
Brioche behind Ballymoss in the 1957 St Leger, and two
years later won the Doncaster classic on bookmaker William
Hill's good filly Cantelo.

He has ridden so many good races, that we are inclined to
take him for granted. We have come to expect the highest
standard of skill, competence and integrity and he never lets
us down. In 1967 he rode a beautifully-judged race to win
the Oaks on Pia, the cosmopolitan filly nobody wanted, to
notch up a first classic success for Bill Elsey, whose father
had won the classic with Frieze and Musidora.

By October 1970 Edward Hide was thirty-three years old.
His 1,350 successes included wins on every British racecourse.
Since he had left his Malton home and stud to join Gordon at
the start of the '69 season, he had already ridden nearly 150
winners and the call of the south was strong. Nevertheless he
turned down a most tempting offer with Ryan Price's fast
expanding stable and returned to a £4,000 a year retainer at
Highfield, where he had spent most of his career.

But the second claim on his services was made by Bill
Watts, who had taken over from Walter Wharton at
Richmond. This was to prove the decisive factor. The high-
class horses he now had to ride included Richard Stanley's
lovely filly Waterloo.

After finishing third in her preliminary outing to the
subsequent Two Thousand Guineas winner High Top,
Waterloo was allowed to start at 8 to 1 in the One Thousand.
She looked superb. Edward sat into her until the Bushes,
where he took the lead and had no difficulty in holding off
Sandy Barclay on the French filly Marisela to win by two
lengths.

The virus-cursed flat season of 1972 ended with Edward
Hide third on the list. He rode 105 winners, which was two
more than Lester Piggott, who was busy capturing the
European Championship on the eve of Britain's entry into
the Common Market. Eddie scored 90 seconds and 89 thirds,
so that he was unplaced in only 326 of his 610 races. The
Hide fans know that they always get full value for their
money.

I have always believed that given, say, the Murless retainer
when Warren Place was at its peak, Edward would have been
champion jockey. He has the ability, intelligence and general

FREE
EYE
TESTS
AT Boots
Opticians

...ed from Rommel's headquarters during the war

...view of Hitler's giant horses

...mm shot. Fitzgeorge-Parker tried to tow it, but it was impossible to move. On the return journey, with a wounded man riding on the back, his tank was fired on by its own infantry but managed to reach base intact. He spent time in a comfortable farmyard with, he reported later, some "bomb-happy" hens that bounced into the air whenever a gun went off.

Fitzgeorge-Parker, who always went into battle wearing a white silk scarf,

was awarded an immediate MC. He was subsequently appointed signals officer, and, although wounded in the course of fierce fighting in Italy, he remained in command of his troop.

Early in 1944 the Greys returned to England to prepare for D-Day, and Fitzgeorge-Parker accompanied them in the Normandy landings in June and during the rest of the campaign in north-west Europe. In Brussels he accepted a young woman's invitation back to her flat, but was disturbed to discover, when he opened her wardrobe to hang up his clothes, a German officer's uniform hanging there.

After the German surrender the Greys moved to cavalry barracks at Luneburg, south of Hamburg. Fitzgeorge-Parker retired from the Army in 1949 in the rank of major.

A fine horseman, Fitzgeorge-Parker was a contender for the British showjumping team in the 1948 Olympics; he rode in point-to-points in the West Country, and at one stage the trainer Fulke Walwyn offered him the job of his amateur jockey, but family commitments prevented his accepting.

Instead Fitzgeorge-Parker became assistant to the trainer Atty Persse before, in 1951, setting up on his own at Lambourn, from where he was to send out more than 50 winners on the flat and

over jumps. He had an expert eye for a yearling. One of his horses, Singing Wave, ran at Aintree, but failed to make it round the Canal Turn at Aintree, ending up in the canal itself, to the delight of the press.

Finding it hard to make ends meet, in 1958 Fitzgeorge-Parker gave up training. His first experience of journalism had been starting the regimental magazine at the end of the war; now he became a contributor to *Horse & Hound*, and in 1959 joined the *Daily Mail*, becoming its chief racing correspondent. He was noted for his strong opinions and his talent for picking up exclusives; he also set the newspaper's record, with 11 consecutive winning naps.

In 1971 Fitzgeorge-Parker left the *Mail* to go freelance. He was a *Raceform* columnist for 14 years and wrote for *Pacemaker* magazine and the *Sun*. He also published 24 books, including the popular *Training the Racehorse*.

Fitzgeorge-Parker was the uncle of the trainer Marcus Tregoning, and was immensely proud when his nephew won this year's Epsom Derby with Sir Percy.

With his first wife, Pauline Whinney, whom he married in 1948, Tim Fitzgeorge-Parker had a son and two daughters, one of whom predeceased him. He married secondly, in 1973, Eleanor Attfield; they had a daughter and a son.

Tim Fitzgeorge-Parker

Trainer and racing journalist who won an MC and esca[

TIM FITZGEORGE-PARKER, who died on August 14 aged 86, was a well-known personality in the world of horse racing; after a "good war" with the Royal Scots Greys he enjoyed a brief career as a trainer before becoming a racing journalist and prolific author.

Fitzgeorge-Parker was one of those people to whom stories accrued. In 1946, while still a serving soldier, he was supervising the reconstruction of the bomb-damaged German Derby course at Hamburg when he was asked to help locate bloodstock which had been looted from France by the Germans. The investigation took him to a stud in Schleswig-Holstein where he and his colleague found that a number of huge draught horses had been used to produce "vast liver chestnuts, standing about 20 hands".

When Fitzgeorge-Parker asked what was the point of these "useless animals", he was told by the stud manager that this was a project that had been ordained by the Führer himself: "I was given old pictures and unlimited resources with orders to produce the true medieval Crusaders' horse, so that Hitler, in a suit of shining armour, could ride as conqueror through the streets of London."

Timothy Barclay Fitzgeorge-Parker was born at Chipstead, Surrey, on July 29 1920. He was educated at Loretto, representing the school at athletics, boxing and rugby (he was later a qualified boxing and football referee).

He went on to Sandhurst, where he was reputed to be the last man fully-trained as a cavalry instructor, and in 1939 was commissioned into the Royal Scots Greys, joining his regiment in Palestine.

Fitzgeorge-Parker took part in the Syrian campaign against the Vichy French and served with his regiment – by then a mechanised unit – in the North Africa campaign from Alamein to Tripoli; he recalled that if any of the Greys were sent back to Alexandria, they were given a large flask to fill up with cocktails from the Cecil Hotel.

On one occasion during the desert campaign, Fitzgeorge-Parker got lost while returning to his base; spotting a camp he drove towards it, only to find that it was Rommel's headquarters. He was locked up, but escaped through an open window and stole a Jeep (he always said that he suspected the Germans left the window open on purpose because they did not wish to be weighed down by PoWs).

In September 1943 the regiment took part in the landings at Salerno, southern Italy. On September 9 Fitzgeorge-Parker, then a lieutenant, was an assault troop leader in C Squadron supporting

Fitzgeorge-Parker: took a di[

the infantry in an attack on Monte Corvino airfield.

The infantry were almost at the aerodrome hangers when they were held up by enemy light AA guns. Fitzgeorge-Parker brought up his troop of tanks and quickly knocked out the guns and took 25 prisoners. He then destroyed two tanks a 75mm gun and several smaller guns.

After the troop was ordered to withdraw, his second sergeant's tank was put out of action by an 88-

tumour the "size of a tennis ball" was removed from his stomach, followed by three months of chemotherapy. At times, he was too ill to get out of bed and memories of their adventurous past could not have seemed more distant.

By the summer of 2001, Rob was in remission and the couple decided to rethink their lives. They decided they wanted to quit their jobs in London and attempt the Seven Summits.

"We asked ourselves, 'What is life about? Sitting in an office all day?' And we realised that the most important thing was spending time together," says Rob. "It just so happened that we spent time together being active."

"We'd discussed the Seven Summits before," continues Jo. "But after Rob got better, we decided to stop talking about it and actually do it. We didn't want cancer to put handcuffs on our lives."

Doctors gave them the go-ahead – requesting only that Rob return home for check-ups every four months – and, using their savings and loans, they set off in the summer of 2003.

The couple believe that their experience of cancer prepared them for the gruelling challenge and the hardships they encountered. On Mt Vinson they were trapped in a storm so vicious they feared their tent would be shredded. On Aconcagua, Jo developed tonsillitis at around 20,000 feet, her windpipe closing to the width of a pencil, making it almost impossible to breathe in conditions that were already oxygen-deprived. And in the North Pole they had to contend with several

Reaching the summit was a momentous occasion, not just because they were at the highest point on the planet – "You can see for hundreds of miles, you notice the curvature of the earth and the inky black of space above," says Jo – but also because it was three years to the month that Rob had gone into remission. He was officially clear of cancer again.

"When we got down, it felt pretty amazing," Rob says. "We'd been handed a gift – we were now in the safety zone, and not just because we were off the summit of Everest."

The experience has clearly strengthened their relationship. "I feel we are like a stone-arch bridge, which gets stronger the more pressure you put upon it," says Rob. "We had some pretty horrible times, but also some sublime and exciting ones."

Jo nods in agreement: "I think when you are just surviving, which is essentially what we were doing on those mountains, you learn to appreciate life a lot more."

And for their next adventure? They are planning something even more challenging than Everest: they want to start a family. But children will not inhibit their adventures.

"Oh no," smiles Jo. "We'll just do something a little easier, like sailing across an ocean."

● *'Holding On: A Story of Love and Survival' by Jo Gambi (Piatkus) is available for £15·99 (rrp £17·99) + £1·25 p&p. To order, please call Telegraph Books on 0870 428 4112*

(*Above*) Double Century winning the Sydney Cup. Note the length of the Australian jockey's stirrup leathers. (*Below*) Batchacre Hall, ridden by Ron Barry, leads over the last to win the 1979 Daily Express Triumph Hurdle Race Trial from Hill of Slane (Tommy Carmody).

(*Above left*) Jonjo O'Neill on Alverton being led in after winning the Piper Champagne Cheltenham Gold Cup in 1978. (*Above right*) Sutton Place, Wally Swinburn up, being led into the winner's enclosure after winning the 1978 Coronation Stakes at Ascot. (*Below*) Yves Saint-Martin on Crow.

(*Above left*) Joe Mercer riding Super Asset wins the 1979 Hyperion Stakes from Lester Piggott on Bay Street. (*Above right*) Portrait of jockey Edward Hide. (*Below*) John Francome on Rodman taking the last fence ahead of Linkenholt, ridden by Andy Turnell, who got up to win the 1979 Mecca Bookmakers' Handicap Hurdle at Kempton.

(*Above left*) Tony Murray with Dickens Hill being led into the winner's enclosure after winning the Eclipse Stakes at Sandown. (*Above right*) Lester Piggott in action. (*Below*) The 1979 Fellcourt Handicap Steeplechase at Lingfield. The winner Lochage, ridden by Graham Thorner, leads at the final fence from Fjord (A. Webber) who was second.

(*Above*) Steve Cauthen riding Cracaval gets the better of favourite Ile
de Bourbon, ridden by John Reid, in the 1979 September Stakes at
Kempton Park. (*Below*) Jockey Paul Cook.

(*Above*) Northern Baby, ridden by Philippe Paquet, wins the Champion Stakes at Newmarket from Willie Carson on Town and Country and B. Taylor on Haul Night. (*Below*) Joe Mercer on Masked Marvel.

(*Above*) In the 1979 Whitbread Gold Cup Bill Smith on Diamond Edge leads over the last to win from Master Smudge (R. Hoare). (*Below*) Ringgit (right), ridden by Lester Piggott, winning the Rookery Handicap from D. McKay on Grand Conde. Wally Swinburn on Gypsy Castle was third.

(*Above left*) Pat Eddery is led in after winning the 1978 Jersey Stakes at Ascot on Camden Town. (*Above right*) Steve Cauthen.

(*Right*) Willie Carson.

outlook. Furthermore, his somewhat shy, self-effacing manner belies great determination and dash. He rides every type of course equally well and it is significant that Chester with its tight bends is, and always has been, one of his favourite tracks. Like Lester he shines on the Roodeye and, also like 'the long fellow', he rides that totally different, wonderful other northern course, Doncaster, brilliantly.

In 1967, however, a typically unselfish decision by Eddie won the £6,583 Lincoln Handicap for his father. He decided, entirely off his own bat, to forego the ride on Ben Novus in the year's first big flat race.

Instead of putting up over-weight, the course specialist watched from the stands as Peter Robinson took the lead a furlong out and drove the black five-year-old for a splendid victory.

Eddie, who had ridden the horse in nearly all his previous races, would have ridden him in the Lincoln if he had been able to do the weight of 7 st 10 lbs. 'I ride at 7 st 13 lbs', he said, 'and, while I might have risked one pound overweight, it would not have been fair to put up any more.'

So six weeks before the race Eddie and his father engaged Peter Robinson, who had previously won the Lincoln on Marshal Pil and Mighty Gurkha. And they were able to tell the owner, Irish veterinary surgeon John Peatt, who had just retired after twenty-six years' practice at Leominster, that his 300-guinea bargain purchase had a great chance of winning.

'I have been backing my horse ever since then,' said Peatt. 'When I saw my green colours a furlong from home, I knew I was going to win. It is by far my biggest success. Robinson rode him just like Edward.'

There was a happy postscript five years later, which surprisingly escaped the Press at the time (possibly because I was still in limbo between leaving the *Daily Mail* and joining the *Sun!*)

When Peter Robinson, then a trainer, required a jockey for his strongly fancied Sovereign Bill in the Irish Sweeps Lincoln he offered the ride to Eddie who had won the race on Double Cream the previous year.

Sovereign Bill opened at 13 to 2 but was backed down to favourite at 9 to 2 in an infectious gamble. A quarter of a mile from home he was hanging badly to the left, but Eddie coolly straightened him, took the lead and rode him out strongly to win by three-quarters of a length from Dowdstown Charley. Peter had repaid the favour. There can have been few more satisfactory endings.

Bill Watts, who had started training in 1968, recalls: 'Susan Stanley leased Waterloo from her husband, Richard, who had bred her at his New England Stud. As a yearling the filly was so small and backward that she got tired after her lad had been riding for ten minutes and had to be led home from canters! As a two-year-old she grew and grew. When I got back from my winter holiday I found the sheep had grown into a ram!'

As might be expected, Edward and the bold chestnut filly struck up an excellent understanding and enjoyed a comfortable victory on her first racecourse appearance in the Wilkinson Memorial Stakes at York, where they took the lead two furlongs from home. The going was firm.

It was just the opposite for her next outing in the Queen Mary Stakes at Royal Ascot, where the ground was really heavy — so heavy in fact that, because starting stalls could have wrecked the precious turf and even got stuck, they were dispensed with and all races were started by flag.

'It was so bad', says Bill, 'that we nearly decided to withdraw her.' He needn't have worried. He had the right jockey. The 'Cock o'the North' was no stranger to such conditions. Edward got a good break and, sitting into his filly, holding her together and keeping her perfectly balanced as she galloped through the mud, made nearly all the running to win unchallenged by six lengths.

However, it was not all plain sailing for Bill Watts in that first year after moving from the Pegasus yard in Newmarket to Richmond. He had another good two-year-old called Winter King with whom he won the Scarborough Stakes at York and then again at Haydock.

'There was nothing between him and Waterloo,' he says. 'And father always told me: "If you can't separate them, they're none of them any bloody good!"'

Winter King, unhappily, injured himself so badly on a subsequent occasion that he had to be put down.

Now they decided to take Waterloo to France for the Prix Robert Papin at Maisons-Laffitte in the middle of July. Drawn badly on the rails, she was beaten into fifth place behind Sun Prince and Deep River.

Her next outing was the Lowther Stakes at the York Festival Meeting in August. Bill says: 'There were just three runners. Edward and I thought it was a formality, that Waterloo would canter in. So did everyone else. We were 2 to 1 on favourite.'

Once again the chestnut filly, who looked superb, jumped out of the gate and tried to make all the running, but when Rose Dubarry came at her two furlongs out, she had no real answer and was beaten two and a half lengths.

Now the Stanleys and their young trainer were really worried. 'We had to sit down and think,' says Bill. 'Really thrash it out. We decided that we would change tactics and hold her up instead of allowing Waterloo to make all the running as she had done hitherto. Now we would hold her up for a late run.

'We told Edward and, I must admit, he thought we were crackers. But he did what he was told. He taught her to settle down really well and, when we took her to Ayr for the Harry Rosebery Challenge Cup, he held her up and brought her through with a late run a furlong from home to win impressively.

'A fortnight later we took her to Newmarket for the Cheveley Park Stakes. Edward repeated the performance exactly and, coming through at the Bushes, went on to win nicely from a good field of sixteen other fillies. We were satisfied. She'd done enough for the season.'

It was an empty horsebox that travelled back to Yorkshire. Waterloo had remained in Newmarket for a two months' rest at her old home, the New England Stud. Bill Watts picked her up again and brought her back to Richmond from the December Sales.

That was a terrible winter in Yorkshire — cold and wet. It was so wet that Bill Watts could not get his horses on to the gallops until the end of January. The days sped by and Waterloo was still confined to walking and trotting on the roads.

Says Bill: 'I absolutely despaired over the going. It was a terrible time for us. I couldn't do any work with my horses and there was the One Thousand Guineas coming closer and closer.'

Waterloo was now a very big filly. She was so robust that she looked more like a colt. Indeed, when, out of interest,

Bill had all his horses tested, he found that Waterloo contained far more male chromosomes than any other filly in the yard. Susan Stanley told me at the time: 'She was much more masculine than any of the other fillies.'

For me this confirmed a long-held suspicion about the reason for the greatness of the classic race-mares and for their bad breeding records. Perhaps it explains why so many outstanding fillies have bad, masculine heads. Not, I hasten to say, that this applied to Waterloo.

This intelligent enterprise of a first-class young British trainer uncovered a hornets' nest which had been lying dormant since some Russian women athletes were found to be intersexed.

Should such fillies be allowed to compete against normal members of their sex in prestige classic races, heavily endowed by owners and punters, to prove their worth as the mothers of future generations and so to strengthen the breed? Could it not be a waste of the race and all that money if a masculine filly wins? At a time when classic winning fillies are fetching sums well into six figures, these questions must surely be answered. Perhaps pre-race sex tests should be carried out as in the case of female competitors in the Olympics?

When I told leading horse veterinary surgeon Alistair Fraser about the Waterloo test, he said: 'That's started something!' He added: 'Certainly some horses, like humans, are born intersexed. And it's quite possible that a filly with an unusually high quota of male chromosomes could be a super-female like the Russian athletes.'

'What about hormones?' I asked.

'That,' said the famous vet, 'is very different and could present a major security problem, involving phenomenal expense. It makes me shudder. Sex hormones can be introduced artificially and could affect performance. They could well be very successful on racehorses.

'If they do work, they would be wonderful from the criminal's point of view because there is no means of testing for the presence of artificially-introduced hormones. The only way you could prove anything would be to catch a man in the act of administering it.

'There are so many different hormones, such as cortizone, progesterone, testosterone, which have a remarkable effect in conditioning horses fast.

'Geldings, in particular, can be fantastically improved by testosterone, the hormone they lack, because it is normally produced in the testicles. It has nothing to do with fertility but it is the one which in a human male produces whiskers and with old men revives virility.'

The quantity of chromosomes in an animal remains constant throughout its life. But hormones are chemical substances and the amount of them circulating in an animal's or human's body varies from moment to moment.

For example, if you are driving along at considerable speed and come round a corner to find your way blocked by a herd of cows and somehow, miraculously, you avoid them and come out safely at the other side, then, as you pull up to take a breath, your adrenalin content will be enormously high — far higher than your usual count. If, on the other hand, a high count had been brought about because a natural hormone had been artificially introduced, it would have been impossible, at one time, to prove this fact.

Dr Edouard Pouret, former President of the French Veterinary Surgeons, told me: 'Of course, clever trainers have been using them for years. They are untraceable and very successful.'

However, in recent years the Jockey Club analysts achieved a major, world-shattering breakthrough when they discovered how to test for the use of artificial hormones — otherwise known as 'anabolic steroids'. I believe that it is high time that this brilliant technique was applied to show-jumpers and three-day-event horses, many of whom are boosted either by the pain-killing drug butozolodine or by anabolic steroids.

In my book, cruelty to animals for gain is a very serious crime. And cruelty is undoubtedly involved here, because, although they may look lovely — fit and full of fun and fire as they gallop and jump around watched by the television cameras — the vast majority of these stars are unsound. But their nerves and sensibilities are deadened by 'bute' or anabolic steroids, which allow them to do things and take chances that they would never otherwise do if they had any feeling in their limbs.

I have personal experience of this. When I badly injured my shoulder in a recent heavy fall, the doctor put me on 'bute'. The excruciating pain, which as most horsemen know is peculiar to shoulders, was deadened so effectively that I actually slept on the offending shoulder. But when I awoke the effects of the drugs had diminished and I was in sheer agony. I realized, as I reached for the pill-bottle, that in my un-nerved state I had done far more damage to that shoulder than I would ever have done without the 'bute'.

Not so long ago I was told, by a very famous vet, of a horse that had been competing in Ireland as a member of an international team. It had performed really well. But a fortnight later, when it arrived back in England, the poor creature was in a sorry state. The vet told me: 'He had been off the drug all that time and when we went to get him out of the horsebox, he was down and in terrible pain. So bad was he that we had to drag him out and shoot him there and then.'

That is the effect on horses of 'bute' and anabolic steroids. And we call ourselves an animal-loving nation?

But this digression, about which I feel so strongly, is a long way from Waterloo and her trainer Bill Watts and jockey Edward Hide who struggled against all the odds to attain supreme fitness in that rain-sodden spring of 1972.

Bill says: 'I worked her on Harry Peacock's old Richmond racecourse gallops but before the first classic trial I had been unable to get much work into her. Every time we galloped, I had to send the lads out to tread in.

'So she was still very burly when she arrived at Thirsk to take on High Top. Understandably she blew up three furlongs out and finished third to Bernard van Cutsem's good colt, who was subsequently to win the Two Thousand Guineas.

'But of course I didn't know that then. I was very worried indeed. She should have lasted longer. I had only twelve days to go before the One Thousand Guineas and I was terrified that she would not be ready.

'For her final preparation I gave her one good gallop over a mile giving weight to old handicappers. Edward and I discovered that the race at Thirsk had brought her on tremendously and she worked really well. On the morning before the race we gave her a sharp four-furlong spin.

'When we set off for Newmarket, we knew at last that we had made it. It had been touch and go, but we'd done it. She was really fit and we were confident. Waterloo had come to hand, despite the cold and damp. By the beginning of April she had her summer coat.

'Edward had made his run half a furlong too soon in the Cheveley Park. So now I told him to wait until he was really ready, and then count three before going. At the top of that Newmarket hill our filly was behind a wall of horses and I was frightened that she would not get out. I needn't have worried. As Rose Dubarry burst from the pack, Edward on Waterloo coolly followed her. Coming into the Dip they fairly flew past Rose Dubarry and half way up the hill were two lengths clear. She won easily by that distance from Marisela, with Rose Dubarry a neck away third.

'I had watched the race from the top of the members' stand with Michael Stoute. My heart was in my mouth. As Edward made that winning run, I shouted myself hoarse. So much so that an old lady remarked loudly: "That man's making a terrible row!"

The greatest day in the life of the young trainer ended with a family party at Bedford Lodge, Newmarket, with his mother and father, the Hide family, and the winning owner, Susan Stanley, 'We were very happy,' says Bill simply.

Edward had to wait only a year before realizing every jockey's ambition and writing his name in the history books as the winner of the world's greatest race, the Derby at Epsom. In this, the Shropshire lad's next classic triumph, he was also able to achieve an incredible record double for Arthur Budgett — breeding, owning and training two Derby winners out of the same mare. That loyal, charming horseman had bought Windmill Girl as a foal for one thousand guineas. He then tried to sell her for six thousand guineas but failed. He trained her to finish second in the Oaks on a day when the rain, draining to the inside of the Epsom course, had made it essential to race right under the stands in order to get reasonable going.

Hugh Lupus and his son Heathersett were brilliant but unlucky colts. Hugh Lupus injured himself exercising before the Derby and was prevented from running, and Heathersett, the obvious favourite, was involved in the eight-horse pile-up on Tattenham Hill. His foal from Windmill Girl, Blakeney, was offered for sale by Arthur for only six thousand guineas but he too failed to attract the right buyer and Arthur decided to keep him in training in partnership with his owner, Horace Renshaw. Blakeney won the Derby, and is now standing at the National Stud where he is siring classic winners and perpetuating the wonderful Djebel male line.

Arthur decided to keep the chestnut half-brother by the Ribot stallion Ragusa for himself, after so many failures in the market. However Morston was so backward that he was impossible to race as a two-year-old and, as so often happens, he became in consequence a trifle colty.

The following year he showed tremendous promise and hopes ran high, even though the colt had a lot to make up. But in a gallop at Whatcombe at the beginning of May, it looked as though all might be lost. 'He tried to grab another horse', says Arthur, 'to savage him. I knew his ability and I was really heartbroken.'

Into this crisis stepped his right-hand man, Tom Dowdeswell, one of racing's greatest backroom boys, who had engineered the Derby victories of Windsor Lad, Tulyar and Blakeney, first as travelling headman and later as headman.

At the time Arthur told me: 'Tom is the most superb horseman. But, after all, he is sixty-three years old and I never ask him to get on all the awkward animals that need straightening out. It just wouldn't be fair.'

He did not need to ask Tom to ride Morston. Arthur said: 'Tom, sixty-three years and all, came to me and said he would like to ride the colt. He rode him from that moment onwards and Morston never looked back. He won his Lingfield race and then the Derby. Tom straightened him out so well that, although he showed his race at Lingfield, he did not turn a hair after the Derby. It took nothing out of him. Of course Edward Hide rode him as tenderly and as beautifully as you might expect from such a great horseman.'

At Epsom Morston put up a really magnificent performance for a horse making only his second appearance. He had twenty-four rivals and he started at 25 to 1. But Edward always had him nicely placed, made steady headway down the hill, took the lead at the distance and, keeping the big colt perfectly balanced, rode a powerful confident finish to defeat the Epsom maestro, Lester Piggott, on Cavo Doro by half a length.

Ragusa, that gallant little son of the recently deceased Ribot, had just died himself. Arthur had already turned down half a million pounds from Australia for Morston. Unhappily the big colt slightly sprained a tendon in August and was unable to run again but has now retired to stud where he is proving himself a top-class stallion.

Edward's next classic success came in the 1977 One Thousand Guineas on Peter Easterby's attractive bay filly Mrs McArdy. Travelling strongly on the bridle most of the way in the mile classic, she went clear in the last furlong to win with great authority from Freeze the Secret trained by Luca Cumani. As a result this delightful, so-skilful young Italian trainer called his lurcher dog Easterby. 'Then when I'm feeling really annoyed, I can kick the dog!' he says, laughing.

This was, of course, a Northern success. Mrs McArdy was trained at Malton near Edward's home and stud. But his next classic triumph was to come from Newmarket where he was riding in 1978 as first jockey to Clive Brittain and his chief owner, Captain Marcos Lemos, the tall Greek shipping director with an outstanding war record whose enthusiasm for British racing has been one of the happiest features of the past twenty years.

The Captain has spent a great deal of money on British racing. Ironically, as we have seen, it was Edward Hide who denied him victory in the Derby with Cavo Doro, the Sir Ivor colt who now stands at his Newmarket stud. Nevertheless, by September 1977 no horse had carried the blue and white Lemos colours first past the post in a classic race.

And it was Edward with his vast experience and horse-sense who played a bigger part than most jockeys in achieving that first classic success.

Clive Brittain told me: 'Every year the Captain likes to buy one good-priced yearling around 40,000 guineas at the autumn sales. He picked them out himself. He has a very good eye for a horse.

'He is very keen on a stallion pedigree. It was at the 1976 October Newmarket sales that he saw a lovely bay colt walking around on the exercise ground, followed him back to his box, and determined to try for him, particularly when he discovered that this was the full brother to Juliette Marny, winner of both the Oaks and the Irish Guinness Oaks the previous season.

'Now I know that in theory full brothers and sisters of great horses are no good. You know the saying: "Lightning never strikes twice in the same place." '

But we thought of Dante and Sayarjiaro and, of course, Blakeney and Morston. And Clive said: 'This Blakeney colt from Fonthill Stud was a real beauty. After all, not only had his sister won two classics, but being by Blakeney, it was also a real classic stallion pedigree.

'If he had come up at the Houghton Sales, he must have made treble what the Captain paid. He said he would go up to 40,000 guineas. An agent and Ron Boss were bidding for Arabs. As it approached his price, there were two left in. Then the Captain managed to get that vital 40,000 bid and the colt was ours. We were absolutely thrilled. He was the only horse in the sale for us.'

So the Blakeney colt came back to Carlburg where he was named Julio Mariner. Said Clive: 'He was easy to break. Very quiet and well-mannered. But Blakeneys are slow learners and he was no exception. As a two-year-old we knew he had tremendous ability, and when the Captain went off on his yacht to the Greek Islands, he was keenly anticipating his colt's first run. I had to send a weekly report.

'Julio Mariner had been through the stalls at Newmarket and I thought he knew plenty when he went to York for his first outing in the Acomb Stakes at the big August meeting, ridden by our stable-jockey, Edward Hide.'

The trainer remembers how the colt squealed a lot as he cantered down and, after the first four had passed the post, how he could still be heard as he came in — stone last!

'I was horrified,' said Clive, 'but Edward reassured me. "Don't worry," he said. "I've never ridden anything so green. He never stopped shouting!"'

'So that evening I talked to the Captain on his yacht. I could hear the sound of the sea in the background. It was not an easy message to put over. "We finished last," I said. "But don't worry, he'll be all right."

'It might have bothered other owners. Not him. The Captain has infinite patience and understanding. All the same, I was quietly just a bit worried myself. I went through the *Timeform* ratings of every runner in the race and thought that our colt would have to improve a hell of a lot to be any good.

'But Edward was proved right when we went back to York for the seven-furlong Sancton Stakes later in the month. Not missing his break this time, he took the lead two furlongs out and ran a little green in front. Edward didn't knock him about and, after an exciting battle in the last furlong, he was beaten on the nod a short head by Henry Cecil's Tannenberg. He'd run a terrific race.'

Now owner and trainer were certain they had a really top-class colt. So they went to Ascot for the Royal Lodge Stakes full of confidence only to be disappointed. They finished fourth, eight lengths behind Shirley Heights. Back to York again for the Leyburn Stakes over a mile and he showed what a really good horse he was, winning by seven lengths.

Clive continued the story: 'Finally,' he said, 'we went to Doncaster for the William Hill Futurity at the end of the season. He got into a bit of trouble early on, came late on the scene, was catching the winner fast, producing a great turn of foot, and was only just beaten on the line. We thought that must be the way to ride him.'

Edward said: 'We'll bring him back here to Doncaster next year to win the St Leger.'

During the winter Julio Mariner woke up. The formerly docile colt became quite a handful. Hope ran high in the Lemos-Brittain-Hide camp. But, although he finished second to the subsequent Derby winner Shirley Heights in the Dante and won a minor condition race at York in mid July, the first part of the 1978 season was disappointing. Clive blames himself for two of the colt's poor runs. Owner, trainer and jockey held councils of war. They finally decided to go for the Leger.

Clive says: 'I thought that the best race he had run was probably the Futurity when he came from behind. So we decided to drop him right out, settle him and use his turn of foot.

'I worked him over 1¼ miles on the Stanley House gallop with Celestial Gem and the four-year-old Remezzo, a top-class handicapper who won three good races during the season and who was a hundred per cent reliable at home. I put a seven stone eight lad on his back and Edward rode Julio Mariner.

'I gave Julio Mariner an impossible task. On the final bend of that tight gallop Edward left him fifteen lengths to make up on Remezzo. He was not to move until that bottom turn. I have never seen a horse show such speed. He fairly ate up the ground in those last two furlongs.'

So, despite everything, they were feeling quite confident when they set off for Doncaster. Julio Mariner was one of the rank outsiders of the party and, indeed, started at 28 to 1.

As the field began to go into the stalls at the St Leger close to the stands, the French horse Easter King came down and had to be destroyed. It was an unhappy incident, which was witnessed by millions of people on their television screens.

Clive takes up the story: 'I was worried that this delay would stir him up, but my headman, Mick Leaman — a superb horseman who had come with me from Sir Noel Murless and who rode Julio Mariner at exercise — ran across, caught hold of the colt, led him round and soothed him. He was possibly the calmest of all the horses down there at the start. I was a little afraid that once they were loaded up they might go too fast. Then they could get strung out.

'But I was still very confident as I watched from Phil Bull's box in the stand. As they reached the top turn we were still well in the rear with only three horses behind us and that was the position as Julio Mariner entered that long Doncaster straight. But when I saw him there I said to Phil: 'We're in there with a great chance.'

'Edward picked his horse up now, quietly, and was always going to win from the turn for home. One and a half furlongs out he decided that Julio Mariner was going so well that it was time to go. Possibly he went too soon and our colt showed tremendous speed and went right away and stayed on. It was a tremendous moment for the Captain and me. We had won our first classic. After all the money and enthusiasm that he had poured into the sport, he had really got a just reward at last.'

As I write, Edward has decided to leave Newmarket. He is returning to Yorkshire to ride once again as first jockey to Bill Watts. We'll leave him there as one of the greatest, most popular 'Cocks o' the North' there have ever been.

4

Steve Cauthen

A star is a star in any language and those who saw America's eighteen-year-old making his debut in the Salisbury mud at the start of the 1979 flat season should have recognized the 'supernova' that had burst into the British racing firmament.

From Tod Sloan and Danny Maher through Brownie Carslake, Scobie Breasley, George Moore and Bill Williamson we have come to know that a true horseman can make the grade in any country. That is what 'the Kid' is. Kentucky-born, he had been riding before he could walk.

Good farriers are scarce enough these days, God knows. A blacksmith who is also a first-class horseman is a *rara avis* indeed. But Steve's father, Tex Cauthen of Walton, Kentucky, is just that. When his eldest son decided at the age of twelve that he wanted to be a jockey, Tex set about forging a career for his son that was to take the sporting world by storm.

Within two years of riding his first winner on Red Pipe, trained by his uncle at Riverdowns, a small track near his home, Steve had achieved more success in a shorter time than any other jockey in turf history. In 1977 his mounts won an incredible six million dollars.

When I see some of Britain's leading jockeys of today clumsily fumbling with their whips, I am reminded of the superior style of their predecessors like Steve Donoghue, Sir Gordon Richards and George Moore — those dedicated artists to whom 'pulling it through' was an art in itself. It was all part of that most essential asset of all horsemanship, balance. The old masters taught that you must never raise your whip above the knee — and they never did. They would have been sacked by their trainers if they had. As a young amateur rider in my teens I remember the pride with which I learnt to twiddle the whip through the fingers of both hands and, with the reins tied to the end of my bed, to ride a finish, pulling my whip through faster and faster as practice endeavoured to make perfect.

Tex Cauthen ensured that his son, who was completely dedicated, practised and practised riding bales of hay in a hay-loft. The reins were attached to the wall and young Steve truly achieved perfection in this vital art.

One of the saddest features of the British racing fraternity, excluding a number of top-class trainers but including the majority of the Press, is the insane conviction that British jockeys must be the best. These self-appointed pundits completely ignore the fact that the Americans have our measure, as we know all too well, in show-jumping and polo, let alone in other sports like golf and tennis! In 1978, when Bill 'the Shoe' Shoemaker came over and gave Hawaiian Sound fantastic rides in two Derbys at courses that he had never seen before, Epsom and The Curragh, the media chose to look the other way. They expressed surprise, but no more. They ignored the fact that most of our big races are being won by horses bred in the United States and that the Americans, racing for such huge Tote-monopolized prize-money, do not put mugs on their horses.

Indeed ignoring things they don't like, looking the other way and sweeping anything distasteful under the carpet are all too common as traits of British racing people. A perfect example, relevant to this chapter, occurred in 1972. Vincent O'Brien's Roberto, ridden by Lester Piggott, had just touched off Ernie Johnson's mount Rheingold in the Derby. After an abortive run in the Irish Sweeps Derby at The Curragh, the American-bred colt returned to the fray in the Benson and Hedges Gold Cup at York on 15 August. His opponents included four-year-old Brigadier Gerard, putting his fantastic unbeaten record on the line again, ridden by his regular partner, Joe Mercer, and Rheingold now ridden by Lester Piggott, who was later to partner Barry Hills' fine big bay to victory in the Arc de Triomphe. Roberto was ridden by Panamanian ace Braulio Baeza, one of the very top jockeys in the United States but virtually unknown on this side of the Atlantic. By the same token, of course, Baeza was quite unfamiliar with the European racing scene and in particular with big wide galloping tracks like York. The betting market was significant. It was 3 to 1 on Brigadier Gerard, 7 to 2

Rheingold and 12 to 1 Roberto. What a price about a Derby winner and what an insult to his rider!

Conditions were ideal for the Brigadier: good going and no wind to speak of. The race was a formality but not the sort that the public had expected it to be. Braulio Baeza had Roberto smartly out of the gate and lay up on the pace throughout. Crouched low, steamlined over his horse's withers, he took the lead soon after entering the straight and drove Roberto on to the line to win by three lengths from Brigadier Gerard. Piggott on Rheingold was an ignominious fourth. Not only had Roberto beaten the Brigadier conclusively over his best distance on strictly weight-for-age terms, but he had shattered the York course record for 10½ furlongs by nearly two seconds. His time, 2 minutes 7.10 seconds, still stands unbeaten to this day. It had been a perfect example of brilliant jockeyship and judgment of pace. But it was looked on as a sort of unfortunate fluke and, as everyone tried to find excuses for the beaten horses, it was soon conveniently forgotten. But it was no fluke. The clock does not lie and Brigadier Gerard must be said to have run up to his very best on those figures.

So it was when Steve Cauthen came to England in 1979, pushing on towards his thousand winners; the Kid, not yet nineteen years old, was already a veteran, ice-cool with a built-in clock in his brain and the hands of a great horseman. In two years he had won just about every major American event worth talking about, including the Washington International on Johnny D and America's three classic races, the Triple Crown, on Affirmed. During his record-breaking year Steve had coaxed victory from so many forlorn hopes that punters began to back his mounts regardless. His standing became like that of Sir Gordon Richards during his twenty-five years as Britain's champion jockey, and it was strong enough to give rise to a new word in the American language — 'Cauthenization'.

He had already broken two records of prize-money in a year and of victories in a New York season. Yet the former respective holders of those records, Angel Cordero and Jorge Velasquez, both great American star riders, bore him no resentment whatever. Cordero asked: 'Who could resent a kid like Stevie? He's such a good kid you can't yell even when he beats you.'

And Velasquez, whose record of 299 victories in a New York season had looked unassailable, said: 'He respects people and learns quick.'

When he won the Washington International of 1977 on Johnny D Steve was asked: 'At what stage did you really know you had the race won?' That slow, infectious smile spread over the Kid's face.

'I finally realized it', he said, 'about two days after the race!'

Robert Sangster arranged for Steve Cauthen to come to England in the cold, saturated spring of 1979 when the country was recovering from a very hard winter. He was greeted with excessive bally-hoo which did not trouble him at all, and in totally unfamiliar conditions rode his first English winner at Salisbury for his trainer, Barry Hills. The stories were true. Here was obviously a superb young horseman possessed of charm, integrity, dash, wonderful hands, ice-cool nerve and judgment of pace. But the English pundits couldn't see this. A senior racing journalist said: 'Mark my words! Cauthen will be back in the USA before October. Wait till he tries to ride the English courses against any of our real jockeys trying to outdo him!' Just wait indeed!

The English jockeys had their first real taste of Cauthenization when Steve rode his first classic races at Newmarket. He finished close-up fourth on Topsy in the One Thousand Guineas and then two days later, literally stole the colts' mile classic, the Two Thousand Guineas, on Tap On Wood, a 20 to 1 chance trained by Barry Hills. There can be no greater contrast between the banked turning American tracks and the wide straight Rowley Mile. But all courses and horses seem to come alike to the Kid. Allowing his horse to get perfectly balanced, racing beneath him, he started to make headway three furlongs out. Suddenly inside the final furlong just as Joe Mercer and Kris looked to have the race sewn up, the young American star, who had kept a little in hand, picked Tap On Wood up and produced a final inspired burst which won the day by half a length from Kris with Young Generation just a short head away third. To all of us who had the privilege to be there it had been a demonstration of sheer star quality.

But the knockers were still at work. One of our brightest and most intelligent trainers is Harry Thompson (Tom)

Jones, a great supporter of Steve Cauthen. One day Tom was besieged with constant criticism of the young American from a well-known older trainer who had once been a prominent jockey. After a while Tom could stand it no longer. 'Listen,' he said. 'Do you realize that this lad rode more winners in two years than you rode in twenty!' Collapse of stout party!

Unhappily, as Barry's string was stricken by the dreaded virus, Cauthen's supply of good mounts was limited. So there was no chance of his challenging for the championship.

The year 1979 was a trial by fire, from which the Cauthen steel has emerged tempered and true. His incredible ride in the Two Thousand Guineas warned our jockeys that the stories of Steve's prowess were true. Clearly this did not suit their book and on several occasions only the young American's superior horsemanship has saved him from deliberate disaster which, to their eternal shame, has gone unpunished by the stewards.

On a brighter note, the September Stakes at Kempton had attracted an unusually big crowd because it featured the return of Europe's four-year-old champion, Ile de Bourbon, after a bad attack of virus. The race was thought to be a formality for Fulke Johnson-Houghton's crack en route to a meeting with Troy in the Prix de l'Arc de Triomphe.

But Barry Hills had other ideas. The neat, dapper horseman, whom I rate among the world's top half-dozen trainers, reckoned that his chestnut Cracaval, also a virus-sufferer, was a very good colt by any standards.

Nevertheless it looked all over as John Reid brought Ile de Bourbon with a well-timed run in the straight. To everyone's surprise Cracaval did not give in. Locked together in a thrilling duel, the brown and the chestnut battled right to the line, where Steve just forced Cracaval's nose ahead.

'I thought I was beaten when he came to me,' he said. 'But then I realized that he hadn't much left, whereas I had kept a little bit up my sleeve.'

And that, dear reader, is one of the secrets of the really great jockeys.

Steve rode his thousandth winner on Thousandfold for his boss, Robert Sangster, and finished up as he had started in England, with a winner, on Dame Julian at Sandown. Despite

Barry Hills' virus troubles Steve won 67 races in Europe including 52 in this country. After his return in April we'll be surprised if this charming young man doesn't score at least a hundred in 1980. At last, after nearly half a century, the cry 'Come on, Steve' will be heard throughout England.

5

Willie Carson

William Hunter Carson was born in Stirling on 16 November 1942 — but not into racing. He just became a jockey because he was so small. 'Everyone went on about how tiny I was', he says, 'and joked about how I'd have to be a jockey until I started to believe it myself.'

As a result his parents managed to afford riding lessons for him from the age of twelve with a Mrs McFarlane of Dunblane in Perthshire, who finally got him into racing by writing round to suitable trainers who might have room for a likely apprentice.

Willie more or less tossed up between the three big trainers who replied favourably. He settled for Gerald Armstrong and is thankful that it turned out this way, because, on Gerald's retirement, his indentures were transferred to brother Sam, who had already established a great reputation as a trainer of boys as well as of horses and owners.

This was a very lucky form of education for the lad because Gerald Armstrong, although nothing like as good a trainer as Sam, was an infinitely superior horseman — as out-standing an amateur as you will ever see.

So the half-a-crown-a-week apprentice learnt to jump his horses off, to sit into them until they were truly balanced before asking them for a special effort. Then, driving with ever-increasing power-packed rhythm, he inspired them to produce all their reserves. It is this tremendous attack and this finishing style, so reminiscent of Fred Winter and Stan Mellor, that characterizes Willie and will keep him at the top of his profession for many years to come.

In 1971, when his 145 winners made him runner-up to Lester Piggott, well clear of Geoff Lewis and Tony Murray, Willie was genuinely amazed. 'I can't believe it,' he told me. 'I just have to pinch myself to make sure I'm still awake.'

And when a year later he was being congratulated on becoming champion, he kept repeating: 'I just can't describe how I feel. "The long fellow" must have been taking it easy this year!'

This was not false modesty. It's typical Willie. Like when, after Troy's Derby triumph he put Julian Wilson's topper over his ears — 'just to show my head hasn't swollen!'

He married before his twentieth birthday when he moved down from Yorkshire to Newmarket. 'Both the Armstrongs were tough masters, real pushers,' he said. 'In some ways Gerald was harder, but Sam had a fantastic record with apprentices — he knew enough to he hardest on the ones who were getting ahead. No fun at the time, but I know how it keeps a kid in line. No wonder I finished my apprenticeship without getting big-headed.'

Still, you can't come without a horse and for all his skill, charm and integrity, he might not have become a champion without the retainer as first jockey to Bernard van Cutsem and the wisdom of that splendid trainer in sending him to winter in Hialeah. How well Willie responded. All the tribulations of Crowned Prince's abdication were forgotten and there was a tear in Bernard's eye as his jockey made all the running on the Rowley Mile and powered High Top home in the Two Thousand Guineas, a first classic for both of them, holding off the subsequent Derby winner Roberto by half a length.

Although built in the ideal mould for an international jockey, Willie had taken time to mature and then suddenly blossomed out. Consider the winning figures up to the time when he became champion for the first time. 1962 — one; 1963 — five; 1964 — fifteen; 1965 — thirty-seven; 1966 — thirty-five; 1967 — thirty-five; 1968 — sixty-one; 1969 — sixty-six; 1970 — eighty-six; 1971 — one hundred and forty-five (runner-up to Lester); 1972 — one hundred and thirty-two (champion), and 1973 — one hundred and sixty-three. Champion he certainly was, but the real big time was still just round the corner.

Without doubt the most outstanding single performance of the 1974 season was Willie Carson's remarkable achievement on Nick Robinson's Dibidale in the Oaks. The bare facts of the case are well known. Willie not only remained intact with Dibidale after her saddle had slipped completely beneath her girth, he managed still to ride a pretty vigorous finish which actually got the gallant partnership into third place.

But perhaps the description given by a flabbergasted member of the Press, after viewing the camera patrol film, serves as a more adequate appraisal. 'First the number-cloth fell away and Willie kept riding,' he explained. 'Then the weight-cloth went, but he still kept riding. The saddle goes, but not Willie. He's still pushing as if his life depended on it! I got the feeling that if the horse itself had disappeared from underneath him, he would still have been going strong!'

This was a sad blow for owner, trainer Barry Hills and for Willie, who would dearly have loved another classic success. He did not have long to wait. Barry took Dibidale over to Ireland where she trotted up in the Irish Guinness Oaks at The Curragh.

Although he had lost his title to Pat Eddery, Willie was still going strong in second place with 131 winners at the end of the 1975 season. Then the Christmas lights were dimmed for the lovers of British racing, which suffered a cruel blow when Bernard van Cutsem died on December 9. He was not quite sixty and had finally lost a magnificent personal battle against cancer.

As the end drew near, the ever-immaculate six-footer, now lying wasted in bed, smiled. 'I'm afraid, Carson', he said, 'that I will not be needing you next season. I shall be light enough to ride them myself.'

Bernard is sadly missed. The cool, quiet wit will not easily be forgotten. At Royal Ascot in 1974 he brought off a typical triumphant coup with Old Lucky in the Royal Hunt Cup. After receiving richly-deserved congratulations, the winning trainer was asked by a persistent, eager journalist: 'What are the plans?'

Bernard looked down at him with a pitying expression. 'That was the plan!' he said, and turned on his heel.

At the end of 1976 fate smiled on Bernard's jockey. Joe Mercer, who had been first jockey at West Ilsley for twenty-five years, first under Jack Colling and then under Dick Hern, left the Berkshire stable to be succeeded by Willie Carson. The first Scotsman ever to be British Champion Jockey was now to be Royal jockey in Silver Jubilee year.

Before the season started he had ridden nearly all the

horses in Hern's large string, including the Queen's classic hope, her own home-bred filly Dunfermline — typically well named — by Royal Palace out of Strathcona. This big bay filly had a somewhat plain head but she had tremendous power in her quarters and good depth through the heart.

Although she was still a maiden, Royal Racing Manager Lord Porchester and Dick Hern, with the Queen's approval, decided to run Dunfermline first in the Pretty Polly Stakes at Newmarket.

The Queen, just back from her Silver Jubilee tour of Australia and New Zealand, was able to enjoy one of her few racing days during that particularly busy, memorable year. Her filly and her new jockey did not let her down and I shall always remember Her Majesty's supreme delight as she greeted their return to the winner's enclosure.

Three years earlier, at this same Newmarket Spring Meeting, her filly Highclere had won the One Thousand Guineas but Her Majesty had decided that the French Oaks would be a more suitable target than the Epsom equivalent. How right she turned out to be.

Now, however, Willie, who thought that Dunfermline was still a bit backward and green, confirmed the owner's impression that she would not only stay 1½ miles but would also act well on the Epsom circuit. So it was decided that the Oaks on the eve of the Silver Jubilee celebrations in London would be the filly's next outing.

The Queen was unable to watch that race, but she was at Epsom when Willie rode a sensational race in the Derby on Lord Leverhulme's Hotgrove and was only just beaten by Robert Sangster's The Minstrel, on whom Lester Piggott had to pull out all the stops. Willie, riding the race of his life, had persuaded Hotgrove to run far above his normal form. It was a tremendous performance.

The Queen Mother represented her daughter at Epsom on Oaks day. When he arrived at the course, Dick Hern was told that his jockey had been involved in a car crash on the way, would definitely not arrive in time for the first race and might not even be there for the second. As the Oaks was the third race on the card, Dick and Lord Porchester asked Joe Mercer to stand by.

Happily Willie arrived unhurt and in his usual good form to be weighed out for his classic ride on Dunfermline. Robert

Sangster was expected to complete a classic double by winning the Oaks with Durtal. But, on the way to the start, this brilliant but temperamental filly got loose and injured herself so badly that she had to be withdrawn.

Willie had Dunfermline nicely away and was going well in about sixth place as they galloped up along the back straight. However, as they started to turn, Dunfermline was badly hampered and knocked right back so that with less than six furlongs to go, she was nearly last. Willie was undeterred. Even though he had to make up his ground on the outside, he knew his filly's stamina and set to work in earnest. Coming up the middle of the course, he got within striking distance of the leaders a quarter of a mile from home. Riding for all he was worth, he forced the royal filly up to beat Freeze the Secret by three-quarters of a length. Willie had won the Silver Jubilee Oaks for the Queen. Even at the end of his triumphant 1979 season he still told me: 'That was the greatest moment of my career.'

There was more to come. In the St Leger, which the Queen was once more forced to watch on television, he rode a tremendous race to beat Lester Piggott on Alleged, the Vincent O'Brien colt who was to win the Arc de Triomphe twice in succession. Dunfermline's stamina was magnificent. In more than two hundred years only fourteen fillies have won the Oaks and the St Leger. Three of those were bred at the Royal Studs.

In 1978 Willie regained his title with his highest-ever score of 182 winners. He was well clear of his nearest rivals — Pat Eddery (148), Joe Mercer (114), and Greville Starkey (107) — who enjoyed the best season of his whole career.

Although there were no classics for Carson, he struck up a good relationship with Troy, a strong, handsome, dark bay, two-year-old son of Petingo, on whom he won nine races at Newmarket and Goodwood. Although beaten by Ela-Mana-Mou by a neck in the Royal Lodge Stakes at Ascot, it was clear that stamina would be the forte of this superb-actioned colt. His dam, La Milo, by the St Leger third, Hornbeam, won at around 1½ miles and Troy was half-brother to six winners including the top-class, middle-distance performer Admetus, who was by Reform, and another very useful middle-distance winner, Tully, who was by Tudor Melody.

In 1979 Troy proved himself the best three-year-old colt

in Europe, winning six consecutive races, admirably produced on every occasion by Hern and ridden with skill and understanding by Carson. Willie achieved every jockey's ambition, winning not just the Derby, but the two hundredth running of the world's greatest race. In addition the partnership won the Sandown Classic Trial, the Predominate Stakes at Goodwood, the Irish Sweeps Derby at The Curragh, the King George VI and Queen Elizabeth Diamond Stakes at Ascot and the Benson and Hedges Gold Cup at York. The Derby was the most extraordinary performance put up by this splendidly lazy colt. Willie was hard at work a long way out and somehow brought his mount from a seemingly impossible position in the rear through his field at an electrifying speed to win by seven lengths, the largest winning margin in over fifty years.

So, even if W. Carson lost his jockeys' championship to J. Mercer, he had adequate compensations.

6

Bill Smith

Born in 1948, Bill started riding at the age of nine when his father, a racing cyclist, owned a cycle shop at their Shepperton home close to Kempton Park.

'Neither of my parents rode. But they gave me pets and, through mice, rabbits, guinea-pigs, cats and dogs, I eventually graduated naturally to ponies.' He showed, show-jumped and rode in gymkhanas until he left school at fifteen and went on a month's trial to Fred Rimell's stable at Kinnersley. 'But I was so windy and homesick, that I came home at the end of that month.'

Home was by that time at Hayling Island in Hampshire and Bill took a job as a salesman with Moss Bros., the ubiquitous men's outfitters and clothes-hire firm, at Southsea. 'I learnt a lot. It wasn't like working in any ordinary shop. We had nice customers and I learnt to talk to all the fresh people I met. This did a great deal for me.'

After eighteen months Bill felt the call of the horse and the outside life again and left to work in a riding stables just outside Portsmouth.

'It's a sporting part of the world and I managed to persuade one of our clients to give me a ride in a point-to-point. I had got the racing bug now. I negotiated a few fences and then fell off.'

'But by now I was eighteen, reasonably tall, with a short back and long legs. Next time, in a hunt race at Hackwood Park near Basingstoke, I won, beating one of the first girls permitted to ride against men in English points.'

With his enthusiasm fired, Bill became assistant to the Hampshire trainer, John Stuart Evans. 'I won another point-to-point at Hackwood. But I wasn't very good. Every Sunday morning it was never "How did you get on?" but "Which fence did you fall at?"'

When he was still eighteen, Bill rode his first winner under Rules for John Blake, a permit-trainer, on three-year-old Silver Mead, in an all-aged selling hurdle at Taunton. 'You couldn't get much lower!' He beat a future colleague and stable-mate, Aly Branford, by a short head. It was his only win as an amateur.

'John Blake had horses in training with Bill Marshall, who was then at Ogbourne, near Marlborough. Bill, who had seen me win the Taunton seller, asked me to ride another three-year-old called Harlech Lad for him but insisted on me turning professional first. I won four novice hurdles on that horse and stayed on as the Marshall stable-jockey for four seasons, which produced over fifty winners.'

It was a wonderful chance, which Bill, who always seems to have been in the right place at the right time, seized with both hands. He was soon retained by Bill Marshall, Les Kennard and David Tatlow.

'So I was covering a large area — Marshall for the London meetings, Tatlow in the Midlands and Kennard in the west with such sterling horses as St Patrick's Blue, Stradivarius and Silver Mead, who Bill Marshall had bought, to ride. I even won the Irish Sweeps Hurdle on Kelanne and my present house is called after him.'

He added: 'I never did any schooling for any of them, except one for David Tatlow when I fell off! That was the end of that!'

Bill's not in bad company. It was a joke at Findon that Fred Winter, the greatest of them all, was hopeless at schooling on the home gallops.

Once again fate then took a hand. Bill was getting a few rides for Edward Courage when the stable-jockey, Johnny Cook, broke his leg. 'I won the S.G.B. Chase on Spanish Steps and the Stone's Ginger Wine and Champion Chase on Royal Relief.'

At the same National Hunt Festival Ken White was concussed on the day before the Daily Express Triumph Hurdle. Fred Rimell offered Bill the ride on Zarib — and he won. That April he had his first Grand National ride on Bright Willow and finished seventh.

Towards the end of the season, cantering down to the start at Devon and Exeter, his horse slipped, stumbled and fell, breaking his jockey's left knee and leg. But young bones mend fast and in six months Bill was back, as stable-jockey to Fred Rimell, replacing Terry Biddlecombe.

He stayed at Kinnersley for two seasons and, although it was never the happiest of partnerships, Bill once again seized his chances. The first season he won the Champion Hurdle with Comedy of Errors and rode the giant into second place behind Captain Christy in the Irish Sweeps Hurdle.

Next season they won the Sweeps but were beaten by Lanzarote in the Champion Hurdle. Bill, who won another Champion Chase on Royal Relief at that Cheltenham, was blamed for Comedy's defeat. He says simply: 'The horse was just not right on the day. After three hurdles he couldn't go the pace. He couldn't get there. If he'd been the same horse as he was in the Sweeps, he'd have trotted up.'

When Terry Biddlecombe retired at Cheltenham, Bill started riding for Fulke Walwyn and he began the following season as first jockey for the great Saxon House stable.

It began badly. 'On an outside ride at Fontwell, my horse slipped up on the flat, killing itself, cracking my pelvis and shoulder blade and causing severe internal bruising. It was called Shattered!'

But he was out for only three weeks and, as a highlight of a sketchy season with a sub-standard team of horses, he won the Schweppes Gold Trophy on the Queen Mother's Tammuz.

'One of the best hurdlers I've ever ridden. A tremendous fast, game horse. Such a shame he had bad legs. It was fantastic winning for the Queen Mother. I can't tell you how much it means to me being her jockey. The whole thing of riding for her is just marvellous.'

Another great moment for Bill was at Ascot when he partnered Sunyboy to win the Queen Mother's three hundredth winner under N.H. rules. And, but for two bad mistakes, he reckons that he would have also won the two-mile Champion Chase on Game Spirit for the royal owner.

'Dramatist's first win at Newbury at 33 to 1 had been a real surprise to us all. Two hurdles out I realized that I must win and he cantered in. He impressed me as the only horse I had ever ridden, apart from Comedy, who could make up an immense amount of ground without you knowing it. He just seemed to find an extra gear and lengthen his great stride.'

Bill cannot say enough in praise of Fulke Walwyn, although it took them some time to get to know each other.

'He's a really super fellow. So very thorough. He has a true insight into his horses' characters, feels for them and has infinite patience. He'll try different bits, for example, until he finds the right one for the horse. He'll even school a top hurdler like Dramatist over baby fences, if he thinks it will do him good. We can stop and discuss the horses together. He's so intensely loyal to his horses and to his jockeys that it gives you heart, makes the whole job seem worthwhile.'

Bill has now had four National rides. He finished third and fourth on Spanish Steps. During 1970 and 1971 he had fifty rides on the flat for Bill Marshall and got his weight down to 8 st 5 lb.

'I beat Willie Carson one day on Saratoga Skiddy. It was a super education and I learnt a lot. But it made me a bit "flat-race pretty" and too free with my stick. I'm much stronger now and don't need to pick it up as I used to.'

Ideally made, with strong shoulders, Bill can ride easily at 10 st 2 lb. He bought a house with ten acres at Hambledon in Hampshire, has built an American-style barn with seven boxes and will increase the number to fourteen.

He still carries on show-jumping, trains a few point-to-point horses and looks after a couple for Derek Kent, for whom he rides out. 'A grand little man. He never stops learning and I have learnt a hell of a lot from him. One day I'd love to train. But you need the place, the owners and the money.'

From the way that Bill's career has shaped so far it would be no surprise at all to find fate producing all the necessary ingredients at the right time.

When I staged a show-jumping contest for jump jockeys at Weyhill in aid of the Save the Children Fund, nothing was too much trouble for Bill. He brought down his own top-class horses, superbly turned out, and provided crowd-pulling star riders including Jeff King, Philip Blacker and himself. Of course they won the big prizes. But they richly deserved to do so.

7

Those Frenchmen

Yves Saint-Martin

At the start of the seventies only one Gallic cavalier rang a bell with British race-goers: the neat, dark, handsome Yves Saint-Martin. The French champion, who has won all our classic races at least once, had already been successful in the 1962 Oaks on Monade and the Derby of 1963 on Relko.

At the time of that Derby I had not long given up training myself and, from the start of that season, I was immensely impressed with François Mathet's colt on my visits to France.

My regard was so high that, some weeks before Epsom when he was still a 10 to 1 chance for the classic, I wrote in the *Daily Mail*: 'Relko will win our Derby.' He was soon a hot favourite. Now, Derby Day is enough of a strain for every man and horse concerned, let alone for a twenty-one-year-old Frenchman riding the favourite. But, before the start of the big race, I witnessed the most extraordinary incident, which convinced me that here was one of the finest horsemen-jockeys I had ever seen.

It was dear old deaf Eph Smith who was involved in one of the most sporting gestures ever. At the last moment Eph had accepted a ride in the Derby on a 100 to 1 outsider, Hullabaloo, an unruly colt, who refused to line up at the start. Backing right away from the gate, he indulged in every sort of antic, delaying the start of the classic by a quarter of an hour.

The twenty-four other jockeys rode round or stood by the gate, minding their own business. But twenty-one-year-old Yves Saint-Martin on the hot favourite and eventual easy winner Relko, quietly showed all the signs of a great natural horseman and a most unselfish young man. He rode back to where Eph was struggling with his stubborn mount and tried to lead him back into line. Unfortunately Hullabaloo, living up to his name, refused to take any part and was left. With what cool confidence Yves rode that Derby winner, always in the first three and switching smoothly to the centre of the track two furlongs out to win with contemptuous ease.

The son of a civil servant, Yves was born at Agen, midway between Bordeaux and Toulouse, in September 1941. Although he had no racing background, he was sufficiently impressive even at that early age to be apprenticed to François Mathet, a great horseman, who had been a fine rider over fences, finishing second in the Foxhunters' Chase at Aintree. As an ex-cavalryman Mathet has always been a strict disciplinarian and a stickler for good manners. In young Saint-Martin he had ideal material and the finished product must have delighted that tough, uncompromising trainer in the succeeding years. In addition, at a time when the French jockeys were notorious for their cowboy riding, Mathet taught his pupil to ride like a true horseman, neat and tidy in the classic style.

Yves was only seventeen when he rode his first winner at Soissons in northern France, and only twenty when he won his first English classic, the Oaks, on Monade.

Since then we have watched him win most of our big races including the One Thousand Guineas of 1971 on Altesse Royale (for Sir Noel Murless) and the same classic in 1976 on Flying Water; the Two Thousand Guineas of 1974 on Nonoalco; the 1976 Oaks on Pawneese, and the St Leger of the same year on Crow. These last three classic triumphs in one year were due to the fact that in 1974 Yves had left Mathet after accepting an offer to ride for Daniel Wildenstein, whose horses, including the great Allez France, had just been taken over by Angel Penna. Although he may be the complete master of Longchamp, all courses come alike to Yves, who has been described by some of the finest judges like Scobie Breasley and Paddy Prendergast as the greatest jockey in the world.

Paddy gave me an example of Yves' mastery one day at Longchamp where the French champion was seemingly beaten soon after entering the straight. Like a man carrying a heavy bucket in one hand and then transferring it to the other for a while before switching it back to the original hand now well rested, Yves, whose horse was galloping correctly on that right-handed track on his off foreleg, switched him on to the wrong leg, the near fore, and kept him galloping like that for a hundred yards or so before switching him back, when the animal, like a giant refreshed, ran on to overhaul his rivals and win his race.

'That's true horsemanship,' said Paddy. 'There are precious few riders in the world today who would have the slightest idea how to do that.'

In spite of his limited command of English, Yves is universally popular in this country and no one begrudges him his frequent big-race successes. He is a happy, polished citizen who lives with his wife Michelle, daughter of one of François Mathet's headmen, in a charming house at Lys Chantilly not far from the training grounds.

Freddie Head

'Born into racing' is a phrase used with justification about Lester Piggott and Pat Eddery but neither could be handicapped with Freddie Head, grandson of wonderful Willie and son of France's finest trainer and breeder, the complete bloodstock man, Alec Head.

Freddie was born on 19 June 1947. He went to school at St Germain-en-Laye and later, when his father had left Maisons-Laffitte, at Chantilly. He had his first ride in public at Le Tremblay in April 1964 and finished second on a horse belonging to Suzie Volterra. A few days later he won on Pierre Wertheimer's Zambonga at Fontainebleau and finished his first season with a score of thirty-three winners.

By the end of 1979 he had ridden nearly fifteen hundred winners and been French champion three times. His victories include all the French classics at least twice and the Arc de Triomphe three times; he has also won Irish classics and successes in England at Royal Ascot, Newmarket and Doncaster.

In France Freddie rides in nearly every race on every racing day. But he has never been popular with English racegoers, probably because in the Derby he has been well beaten on heavily-backed colts three times in the last nine years. Let there be no mistake, however, it was bad luck rather than any lack of ability which caused his failure in our premier classic. It was not his fault that Bourbon 'created' in front of the

Epsom stands in the 1971 Derby, nor that Lyphard, fast becoming the world's most sought-after stallion, swerved almost off the course the following year.

He is blamed by British pundits for riding with far too short stirrup leathers. This is part of the somewhat pitiful insular attitude towards our own jockeys that I have described in the chapter about Steve Cauthen. It is proverbially unwise of all those ensconced in glass-houses to throw stones. Let those ill-informed critics note that neither Freddie Head nor any other French jockey rides shorter than their English counterparts. Says Freddie: 'I have very short legs and do ride very short, but not, in comparison to our figures, any shorter than Lester Piggott. That would be impossible.'

Hear, hear and so be it! But, as I have stated before, two wrongs do not make a right and there is no possible doubt that, aping Piggott, nearly all European jockeys ride far, far too short. With Freddie, as with Lester, it is doubly a pity that he insists on riding so short because he is naturally a first-class horseman who has been riding since before he could walk.

Freddie is a particularly likeable chap with the nice Anglo-French wit of his famous family. He married France, daughter of banker Louis Dreyfuss, and they live with their three children in style at Gouvieux near Chantilly.

As a true grandson of Willie and son of Alec, Freddie is a highly-intelligent young man with a fine knowledge of racing and an excellent judgment of bloodstock. So, when his father eventually retires, Freddie will be supremely fitted to take over from him.

Philippe Paquet

The youngest of our three Frenchmen, Philippe Paquet, was born at Enghien in December 1952. His father owned a driving school near the Lamorlaye/Chantilly training grounds, but otherwise the family had no connection with racing.

However, being the right size and build and having been brought up in that racing area, Philippe always wanted to be a jockey. With this aim he applied to his local labour exchange and was posted in 1966 to François Boutin, who had recently set up as a trainer after completing several years as assistant to Etienne Pollet. At that time Boutin had only twenty-four horses. Two years later he was to win the Oaks at Epsom with Henry Berlin's La Lagune, his first runner in England. Now he has one of the biggest and most successful strings in France at Le Mont de Po between Chantilly and Lamorlaye.

When Philippe was fifteen, the stable-jockey was that fine, tough practitioner Gérard Thibœuf, who had ridden La Lagune in the Oaks. It was Gérard who suggested another of Berlin's fillies, Shanghai Lily — who had earlier classic pretentions — as the first mount for the boy in a little race at Compiègne, a provincial track about 50 km (30 miles) from Chantilly. Running completely out of her class, Shanghai Lily made all the running to win and by the end of that year had given Philippe two more successes, one at Fontainebleau and another at Compiègne.

François Boutin really looked after his protégé. Philippe says: 'The great thing is that you can talk to him. He really understands horses and men. He tells you quickly if you've done wrong but always gives his reasons. I am very fond of him.'

Boutin, prematurely grey, full of charm and intelligence, would do well in any walk of life in any country. He sent Philippe for three months' work-riding experience in the United States and later encouraged a trip to Hong Kong where the young French jockey became engaged to Michelle, the delightful daughter of leading trainer George Moore, former Australian champion jockey.

Philippe's big chance at home came in 1974 when he became first jockey to Boutin. Although he missed riding the stable's Two Thousand Guineas winner Nonoalco because, since he had not competed in England, it was natural to prefer Yves Saint-Martin, he won the French Derby, a far greater prize, on Caracolero, his first ride in the Chantilly classic. Now he was winning good races at the big Paris tracks, at Deauville and in Italy, where he took the Gran Premio d'Italia on Elizabeth Couturie's Rivecourt.

At this time Lester Piggott was managing to get on to a number of the better Boutin horses in the most rewarding races and there can be little doubt that, apart from the French Derby, the race which gave Philippe most satisfaction in 1974 was the Prix du Moulin at Longchamp.

The English Guineas winner, Nonoalco, represented the

Boutin stable but once again Piggott, who had won on the colt at Deauville, was given the mount. Philippe rode Mount Hagen, one of Daniel Wildenstein's two runners. The other, Lianga, was given to Freddie Head. It was a great race for young Paquet. Mount Hagen won by three lengths from Northern Taste with Lianga third and Nonoalco last but one of the eleven runners.

In January 1975 he married Michelle, and during that season rode 106 winners, finishing second only to Yves Saint-Martin in the French Jockeys' Championship. But, although at that time a supremely happy bridegroom, he was still being treated as the bridesmaid so far as international racing was concerned.

Towards the end of that year the best horse he rode was Manado, winner of the two-year-old classics, the Prix de la Salamandre and Grand Criterium, which earned him the top rating among French two-year-olds. Nevertheless when Manado came over to contest the Two Thousand Guineas it was Yves Saint-Martin who was given the ride, and was to finish in ninth position on that colt who failed to train on.

And while Philippe won the top staying races in France on Sagaro, it was Lester Piggott who partnered Gerry Oldham's wonderful colt in the Ascot Gold Cup. After only three previous rides in England, Philippe, a nice-looking modest young man, is already very popular among the English jockeys. Thanks to his wife he speaks very good English and his visits to this country, Ireland, Italy, Hong Kong and New Zealand have resulted in his being much more internationally-minded than many French jockeys. He seems to have none of the traditional Gallic excitability in his nature and is essentially a quiet rider with a keen understanding and love for the horses which he rides.

He and Michelle have built a lovely home at Lys near Lamorlaye and only a stone's throw from Yves Saint-Martin and Bill Pyers. He loves gardening, playing snooker and going for long walks in the country with his dog.

So when Philippe won the Champion Stakes of 1979 on the Derby third Northern Baby it was a popular success all round. Few realized at the time that, thanks to the disqualifications of Trepan, this top-class French rider was actually gaining his first success in England. Make no mistake. It will not be his last.

8

Frenchy's Fledglings

Frenchy Nicholson's retirement at the end of the 1979 flat racing season was a major tragedy for British racing.

The son of a professional huntsman, Frenchy had it all. Born in 1913, he served his time first in France, where his father was hunting hounds (hence the name Frenchy), and then with Stanley Wootton at Epsom — a nine-year apprenticeship which produced wonderful results. His style and nerves of steel made him one of the heroes of my schooldays. I shall always remember the thrill when he won the 1936 Champion Hurdle on Victor Norman.

Frenchy completed the other leg of the big classic double on his home course with the Gold Cup on Medoc, trained by that beautiful horseman Reg Hobbs, whose ultra-tall, handsome son Bruce had ridden the little black American stallion Battleship to victory in the Grand National of 1938. This was the year in which Frenchy married Diana Holman, a fine horsewoman whose father, Captain Bill Holman — one of the best polo players in the country — turned out a number of winners from the Prestbury yard which is now occupied by his son-in-law.

In March of the following year their first son, David, was born. He was three when his father won the Gold Cup and only five when he himself received his first prize at a local gymkhana. Frenchy, who had twice ridden four winners in an afternoon at Cheltenham, then decided to set up as a trainer. He took out a licence in 1946 but continued riding as David was to do later, and in 1947 he not only rode Tant Pis to victory in the Imperial Cup but also won the Liverpool Hurdle with Mr Fitz as trainer and jockey.

David, trained by his father, became a top-class, stylish jump jockey. Encouraged by this success, Frenchy remembered how well his former master, Stanley Wootton, had trained apprentice jockeys and turned his attention to the flat. With complete selfless dedication he and Diana have taught boys not only to be first-class jockeys but also to be decent men equipped for life. David, incidentally, is admirably following his father's example with jump jockeys.

So British racing owes a lot to Frenchy, whose successes include star riders Pat Eddery, Tony Murray, Paul Cook, Richard Fox and Walter Swinburn.

Pat Eddery

Pat Eddery was born into the racing game on 18 March 1952. His father, Jimmy Eddery, was Irish champion jockey several times and won the Irish Derby on Panaslipper and the Irish Oaks on Silken Glider. He was one of the pioneers of the Irish classic invasion of England. Although Jimmy did not win an English classic, he rode Panaslipper into second place behind Phil Drake in the 1955 Derby and was third in the Epsom classic on Roistar behind Lavandin and Montaval the following year when English candidates were whitewashed by the French and Irish. Then in 1957 he was beaten inches on Silken Glider in the Oaks won by the Queen's Carrozza, who gave Lester Piggott his first success in the fillies' classic.

Pat's mother was a daughter of steeplechase jockey Jack Moylan, who rode Fly Mask into second place behind Master Robert in the 1925 Grand National. Pat was four when he visited Seamus McGrath's yard at Sandyford near Dublin for the first time and was only eight when his father and uncle Con — a good jump jockey in his day — who were working for Seamus, let him climb on to a racehorse. He left school at thirteen and served one year of his apprenticeship at Sandyford before Seamus telephoned Frenchy Nicholson and the boy was sent to Prestbury, Cheltenham in 1967.

Pat has said: 'When I first got there, Frenchy frightened the life out of me. I just wanted to pack my bags and go straight home to Ireland, but I soon realized that I had a wonderful guv'nor . . . I would advise any youngster who wants to get to the top as a jockey and who is prepared to work really hard to go to him. After all, unlike many trainers, he is a first-class horseman and has the time and knowledge to teach us to ride.'

To this I would say that Frenchy made the time to devote to the boys in his care. Over the years he and Diana were wonderfully conscientious in going to the race meetings where their apprentices were riding.

Pat had about forty mounts in public before riding his first winner, Alvarro, in an apprentice race at Epsom on 24 April 1969. He ended up that first year with twenty-three winners and rode fifty-seven winners from four hundred mounts in 1970, including a five-timer at Haydock. His 1973 total of 119 was remarkable because Lester Piggott did not top the ton until his eighth season.

By now he was stable-jockey for Peter Walwyn. At Brighton races in the summer of 1972 Peter's jockey Duncan Keith found that he could no longer compete with the weight problems that had been plaguing him for some time and decided to retire. That very night Peter telephoned Frenchy and fixed up to retain Pat as first jockey to Seven Barrows for the following season. Neither has had any cause to regret the move. Meanwhile, of course, Pat was still under Frenchy Nicholson's guiding hand. He said: 'When Tony Murray, Paul Cook and I were there we had to work very hard. Up at six o'clock, we'd finish at one and he'd have us back at two-thirty, gardening. At four he'd give you half an hour's break and then you'd have evening stables.

'It may have been tough, but it was worth every drop of sweat. He was always watching you and if you did something wrong he'd tell you. If you did something well he'd tell you too — and that meant a lot.'

Once established with Peter Walwyn, Pat did a lot well. His first classic success came on Polygamy in the Oaks of 1974. 'To say that it was easy would be telling a lie,' said Pat. 'I was always scrubbing, yet what a filly! She really pulled it out when the chips were down.' It was indeed a tremendous, gutsy performance from a filly who had had a very hard race in the One Thousand Guineas, being beaten a short head by the Queen's Highclere. Of course, Dibidale, whose saddle slipped under Willie Carson, was the moral winner of that Oaks. But that still does not detract from the wonderful ride that Eddery gave Polygamy.

That was the year when Pat struck up a perfect understanding with a beautifully-made chestnut two-year-old. He had a white question-mark on his face and a flaxen mane and tail, but Grundy was as tough and genuine as they come.

1975 was a golden year for Peter and Pat. Although defeated in the Two Thousand Guineas by Wollow on the day when the unions made a nuisance of themselves at Newmarket, Grundy won the Irish Guineas, the Derby, and then that never-to-be-forgotten race with Bustino for the Diamonds at Ascot.

Let me say here and now that then, and in all his classic races, young Pat showed the cool judgment and brilliant jockeyship of a veteran. In no way has he ever been out-ridden, even by the old master, Lester Piggott. He has thoroughly deserved to be champion jockey four times.

But even Pat 'can't come without the horse' and in 1978, when the virus afflicted Seven Barrows, he lost his title to Willie Carson. The following year the vile disease struck again. But Pat battled on just the same and, although without his mainstay, he still managed to finish third behind Joe Mercer and Willie Carson. Make no mistake. If the Seven Barrows horses are good enough and well enough, this power-ful, natural Irish horseman will surely be champion again.

Paul Cook

The wheel of fortune turns nowhere more inexorably and less predictably than in racing. Paul Cook's career is a perfect example. Born to a life of domestic service in Cheltenham, Paul did not have far to go to acquire a love of racing. And, when he wanted a job in the game, he just took a short bus ride to Frenchy's yard at Prestbury.

The master soon recognized young Cook's ability and made the most of it. Paul rode his first winner in 1963 when he was seventeen. By the 1966 season he had really arrived. His ninety-three winners that year included the One Thous-and Guineas on Glad Rags for Vincent O'Brien.

I well remember the end of April that year when, twelve days after finishing his apprenticeship, Paul Cook challenged Lester Piggott for the lead in the jockeys' championship with a Newmarket double initiated by his first classic victory in the One Thousand Guineas. Cook, who had been twenty that month, reached his first century of winners the previous August in the record time of less than two years. He had

started 1966 with the coveted job as stable-jockey to the late
Sir Jack Jarvis. His chief employer, that great judge, the late
Lord Rosebery, said: 'The boy rode a splendid race in the
One Thousand Guineas. He had a very cool head. He was
properly brought up by Frenchy Nicholson.'

Paul had displayed patience far beyond his years when
winning the fillies' classic for Virginian Mrs Alice Mills and
Vincent O'Brien after a sad display of temperament by
England's Soft Angels had exhausted her own chance and
badly delayed the start.

From a surprisingly good break Sea Lichen, poorly drawn
on the far side, established such a clear lead that Ron
Hutchinson mistakenly came right over to the stands rails,
thereby losing a lot of ground. Berkeley Springs, a different
filly from her previous outing at Kempton with her tongue
now tied firmly down, looked the winner when she took up
the running at the Bushes.

The 11 to 10 on French favourite Miliza II quickly defeated
Soft Angels but it was Glad Rags, five lengths clear when
entering the Dip, who chased the American filly up the hill
and, ridden with quiet determination, just got in front near
the line to win by a neck from Berkeley Springs with Miliza
two lengths away third. Paul said: 'I knew I had to nurse my
filly and ride her tenderly because she had come amiss in the
morning.'

Incidentally, this was one of those occasions when Vincent
O'Brien displayed his mastery. 'Glad Rags needs good
ground,' he told me. 'Although she came in season that
morning, it was sheer determination on her part that won the
race. I booked Cook a week ago because I thought that, being
small, he would match this filly who is only fifteen hands
three inches high.'

Paul's Derby mount Pretendre was tremendously fancied
by Sir Jack Jarvis to win the Epsom classic. Dignity and
impudence, age and youth were sharply contrasted as
Australian veteran Scobie Breasley and our English youngster
Paul Cook fought a thrilling battle up the final hill in that
1966 Derby. Although beaten a neck on the line, Paul did
not suffer one whit in comparison with the great man. And
Sir Jack Jarvis, who was then seventy-nine years old, had
nothing but praise for his jockey despite his disappointment
over Pretendre's gallant defeat.

Everything was going right for Paul. Paddy Prendergast, for whom he won the Chester Cup, declared him to be 'a really great boy' and predicted great things. The newspapers told Lester to look to his laurels. The public cheered their new favourite home.

But it had all happened too fast, and, when the winners stopped coming, the fickle crowds forgot him. Paul Cook was a has-been at twenty-two. Slowly, and by dint of hard work in eleven different countries, Paul has clambered his way up the ladder again. His wife, Carol, has shared the struggle and the recent seasons have seen them triumphant.

With Brian Swift and Nick Vigors he has established himself as a jockey of real talent and application. And Michael Stoute, no mean judge of horse or man, has shared many of his recent triumphs with Paul, who is now right back where he belongs although, in place of that volatile but brilliant boy who burst on to the scene thirteen years ago, we have a mellower and tougher man — and an inestimably finer jockey.

Tony Murray

Tony Murray is another of those jockeys who was born into racing. I well remember his father, the late Paddy Murray, as a brave, successful jump jockey employed by Reg Hobbs, who trained so many good steeplechasers and won the Grand National with the pony-sized American stallion Battleship ridden by his ultra-tall, charming son Bruce, now a successful Newmarket trainer. Paddy married a Wantage girl and it was only natural for him to entrust his son to his old friend Frenchy.

It was a wise move. Frenchy had schooled this good little horseman to perfection as a top-class apprentice. In his first season, 1966, he rode fourteen winners. Subsequent years produced thirty-seven, thirty-one, forty-four, sixty-nine, a hundred and twelve and a hundred and twenty-two.

These figures would have been even more impressive but for a horrible fall when he was put over the rails out in the country at a Windsor evening meeting. It was a fall which nearly killed him, shattered his jaw and gave him a new tough, resolute look, older than his years but in keeping with his character.

Incidentally, it is extraordinary to reflect that our Jockey Club refused to introduce skull-caps for flat-race jockeys until the late fifties after my good apprentice, Taffy Thomas, had been killed when his head struck one of the concrete uprights when his mount, stumbling, hurled him into the Warwick rails. Apparently the objection from the old brigade of the Jockey Club was that skull-caps 'didn't look nice'.

I have nothing but praise for their successors today, who have finally succeeded in re-establishing a ruling body that, from a disciplinary point of view, is the envy of the world. But many of these old men, clinging like grim death to the power and prestige in their little world of the turf which their noble titles gave them, reminded me of the occasion when that wonderful old trainer Mat Dawson advised the Duke of Portland to put a very highly-bred filly in a selling race. The Duke said: 'Surely it is a pity to sell one bred like this?'

Mat's answer was: 'Well, she is a damn bad specimen of a damned good breed; get out of her Your Grace.' That was a Scotsman's way of dealing with a man or horse when he found them bad. And that's what many of the Jockey Club were in those days — damn bad specimens of a damned good breed.

But the tide was turning slowly and several people reminded those in authority that, in the opinion of most people, a live, plain jockey in a skull-cap looked considerably nicer than a dead, pretty one without.

Looking back to that fall towards the end of July 1968 when his mount, Windy Breeze, crashed into the rails at Windsor, Tony recalled: 'I was put over the rails. I shall never believe it was an accident. My jaw was broken in forty-eight places just like a shattered tea-cup and I was in hospital for seven weeks. I resumed at Lingfield on 25 September and three days later won the Royal Lodge Stakes at Ascot on Dutch Bells trained by Ryan Price. That really cemented the relationship between us.'

So, after riding for Doug Smith, Tony graduated to Ryan Price for whom he won the 1972 Oaks on Ginevra. The success of this very temperamental filly was a triumph for the wonderful horsemastership of her trainer. Tony said: 'She had a hell of a temper, so much so that Lester Piggott said she would kill someone some day. The trouble was getting her fit, for, as soon as she was anywhere near ready, she would go haywire. But Ryan, with his uncanny understanding of a horse's mentality, managed to get her to Epsom fit and sane. I shall never know how he did it.'

That was his first classic winner, but Tony had the good fortune to team up in those years with Ryan's European champion sprinter, Sandford Lad. This big handsome colt, a Doncaster bargain bred by Mrs Anne Grubb at her little Big Acre Stud in Co. Tipperary, won three of his four races as a two-year-old in 1972 and was unbeaten in 1973, cantering away with a five-furlong handicap under ten stone early in July and following up with victories in the King George Stakes, the Nunthorpe Stakes and the Prix de l'Abbaye de Longchamp, which he won easily from Abergwaun and Supreme Gift.

'He had a perfect temperament and was a very easy horse to ride,' said Tony. 'I have always thought he would have done even better over seven furlongs or a mile, but there was more money and more opportunities in sprints and that is what he was kept for.'

The following year Tony struck up a happy relationship with a colt, belonging to Ginevra's owner Charles St George, called Giacometti. He too was unbeaten in his first season when his victories in Tony's hands included the Gimcrack and the Champagne Stakes. The following season they were second in the Two Thousand Guineas to Nonoalco and third behind Snow Knight in the Derby.

There then occurred one of those episodes which have become all too sadly familiar with the name of Lester Piggott. In the St Leger Tony was 'jocked off' in favour of Piggott, who finished second on Giacometti to Bustino. In the Champion Stakes with Lester once more aboard, Giacometti reaped the benefit of his consistency and of Tony's schooling by winning the last Group I prestige race of the season. It was enough to sour off the best jockeys and, believe me, Tony is one of the best.

He continued to ride for Ryan Price for a while longer, but then emigrated first to France and then, after a highly satisfactory period in that country gathering experience all the time, to Ireland where he is now right at the very top of the tree, riding for all the best trainers including Vincent O'Brien and, when he comes over here, we can see that here is a first-class international rider by any standards.

One of his chief rivals in the Emerald Isle brings us full circle to the last of Frenchy's fledglings.

Walter Swinburn

Walter Swinburn started his apprenticeship in 1977, the season when his father, 42-year-old Wally, was champion jockey of Ireland — the same ever-popular Wally who in 1956, when apprenticed to Sam Armstrong, had enjoyed considerable success as my stable-jockey when I was training in Lambourn. Wally chose well for his son. He knew the form — who better? — and sent the boy to learn the facts of life, horsemanship, horsemastership and jockeyship from Frenchy, that great stylist and the finest teacher of all time. As it turned out, Walter is the last of that long line of stars because Frenchy has now retired.

To my great joy Walter's first big-race winner Doogali in the City and Suburban at the 1979 Epsom Spring Meeting was trained at Ayr by Charlie Williams, who had been my travelling headman all the time I was training and, in particular, when Walter's father, Wally, was riding for us. Charlie has always been one of the finest exponents of his craft and richly deserves the success that has finally come his way since he took over from Nigel Angus at Cree Lodge, Ayr.

From the moment that he won that big handicap, it was clear that Walter belonged in the same company as his predecessors with Frenchy. He ended the 1979 season with forty-seven winners and the master himself told me: 'He's a decent lad. One day he'll be an eight-stone jockey. It's early days to say whether he'll be top class. But he's very cool and has excellent hands. Above all, he's a worker and a real trier. I reckon he has a good chance of making the grade. He may be the last, but he could well be the best of them all.' And that, from Frenchy, is praise indeed.

9

A Fine British Team

Greville Starkey

Greville Starkey finished 1979 in fourth position with ninety-nine winners. He was always thereabouts, always the danger man.

1978 was Greville's real 'benefit year', as they say in cricket. That season it was appropriate that he should achieve his first century in the Cottesmore Stakes, named after the famous Cottesmore Foxhounds. Of all present-day flat-race jockeys, Greville, who was born in December 1939, is one of the few real horsemen who is equally at home riding across any country after hounds as he is on the racecourse.

It is equally appropriate that The Nail, winner of that hundredth race at Leicester on 24 October, should have been trained by Harry Thompson (Tom) Jones because Starkey was apprenticed for seven years to Tom, who gave him his first winner on Russian Gold at Pontefract in 1955.

More than two thousand winners later, it is worth recalling how highly his master must have rated this fifteen-year-old boy to give him the ride on a horse which, at this early stage of his career, he regarded so highly. It is hard enough to win races, and trainers (other than trainers of apprentices) who put up boys deserve to be canonized.

It was, of course, Starkey who won the Arc de Triomphe on Star Appeal and earlier the Oaks on Homeward Bound. He is a jockey of the highest order in any company. But over the years, despite his obvious quality, the big race winners have been incredibly sparse and up until the 1978 season his talent was wasted through lack of opportunity. Suddenly it seemed to be allowed to blossom. The opportunities came and Greville took them.

In that year he rode the winners of eighteen Pattern Races

in England and Ireland and his ten Group I triumphs included the great English and Irish classic double, the Derby and the Oaks on Shirley Heights and Fair Salinia. In three of those four wonderful races it was the sheer strength of Starkey's finish that won the day.

Shangamuzo in the Ascot Gold Cup, Fair Salinia again in the Yorkshire Oaks, Devon Ditty in the Flying Childers Stakes and the Cheveley Park Stakes, and Swiss Maid in the Champion Stakes were other Group I successes, all of which add up to a truly magnificent feat of jockeyship. At long last Greville had gained the recognition he had always deserved as a top-class international rider.

But for Greville's superb timing, split-second judgment and dash, Mill Reef's son Shirley Heights would not have won two Derbys and earned a proud place as a stallion at Sandringham Stud.

Brian Taylor

Brian Taylor, first jockey to Ryan Price, is just two months older than Greville. He rode his first winner on Creole at Yarmouth in 1956 when apprenticed to the late Jack Leader, and from that charming sportsman rubbed off not only outstanding horsemanship but also a wonderful disposition, so that the polish and balance which Brian exhibits in his riding are the same qualities that characterize the man.

Tall for a flat jockey, the pipe-smoking, hunting and shooting horseman so nearly switched to the jumping game but he persevered and got his much-deserved break when retained by John Winter, with whom he enjoyed a long and successful association.

He won the Derby on Snow Knight in 1974 and that performance set the seal on his reputation as a world-class jockey. He has done everything to live up to it since, particularly as his riding of the Price string has been a feature of the last few seasons.

1976 was a great year which he wound up by winning the November Handicap at Doncaster on Gale Bridge. In finishing third in the jockeys' table with 106 winners, Brian had enjoyed his best year by far. Let us hope that 'Ernie' — as he is often known — remains with us, gracing the racing scene, for some years to come. But how I wish he would let his stirrup leathers down and go back to the length he rode with Jack Leader!

Philip Robinson

In 1969 Prince de Galles, then a three-year-old, landed a great gamble in the Cambridgeshire. He repeated it the following year with 9 st 7 lbs, backed on the day down from 10 to 1 to 6 to 1 second favourite.

The trainer was former jockey Peter Robinson and the rider was the irrepressible farmer, Frank Durr. On several occasions Peter had expressed to me his tremendous admiration of his friend Frank, one of the most popular jockeys of our time.

Eight years after that second Cambridgeshire triumph Peter Robinson died in his car on the way back from racing. With him was his seventeen-year-old son Philip, a grand brainy lad, whom his father had already trained so well as an apprentice that, before his death, he had the joy of seeing him in the winner's enclosure.

As luck would have it, Frankie took the decision at the end of that season to retire from the saddle and start training from the Newmarket yard of his old friend Peter. He proved a quite outstanding first-season trainer and it was not just loyalty and the memory of Peter that made him take young Philip along the road to success with him. He recognized a potential champion jockey and, with no fuss, happily set about continuing Peter's tuition until before long, the boy had ridden all the courses in Britain.

Despite his young age, Philip Robinson is cool and patient beyond his years. He has an inborn judgment of pace and usually brings his winners home with hands and heels since Frankie has told him only to use the whip as a last resort.

Durr has no doubts about his protégé. 'He has a great future,' he says. 'He's very brainy. He has only to ride a horse once and he knows the ABC of the animal. I've seen so many kids who've looked as if they'd make the grade and they haven't got on. If Philip looks after himself, he's going to go on and on and on. Right to the top.'

And by the end of the 1979 flat season, Philip had indeed

scaled the first peak of his career by winning the apprentices' championship from Walter Swinburn. The result hinged on the last few weeks of the season and in the end Robinson came out best by fifty-one to forty-seven.

The future looks good with British race-riding in the hands of young men like Philip and Walter — particularly when there are loyal, knowledgeable men around like Frankie.

10

John Reid

A champion jockey from Northern Ireland? I wouldn't be at all surprised. After all, we've had one from Scotland in the seventies and, for my money, John Reid is championship material.

Born in August 1955, John, a farmer's son from Dromore in Co. Down, was so good with his hands at woodwork that he originally wanted to be a joiner. But, since he had become an accomplished young horseman riding his sister's and his own ponies, and was small and light, he left technical college for a trial run in the racing game. Shrewdly recognizing that there were more opportunities for a good young jockey in England than in Ireland, he was lucky enough to find his way to Major Verly Bewicke at Didcot on the Oxfordshire/Berkshire border.

As an experienced, successful jumping trainer, Verly is a better schoolmaster of horse and rider than many of his flat rivals and was steadily increasing his interests on the level. John was having only his third ride in public when he won the Cucumber Stakes at Goodwood in May 1973 on a filly called Eyre.

Verly brought his protégé along like a good young chaser, helping and guiding but never hurrying so that, just four years later, John rode his 75th winner and so lost the apprentice allowance.

Luck always seems to be a vital ingredient in the recipe for success in racing; being in the right place at the right time can be tremendously important. Some of the stables in the Didcot area are fairly isolated, so that it is not always as easy to find good second jockeys, work-riders as in a centre like Lambourn or Newmarket. One such is Woodway, perched on the side of a hill half-way to the downs high above the little village of Blewbury. Here, from his family home, Fulke

Johnson-Houghton trains good horses well, as his father and mother did before him.

Just at the time when John Reid lost his claim Frank Morby, the quick, capable horseman, who had been working for Fulke, decided to leave Woodway and it was said that the rides would be shared by Lester Piggott and Willie Carson.

John, knowing how sought-after these two jockeys were and, having noticed how well Fulke places his horses to win often at the smaller meetings, seldom frequented by such fashionable riders, had other ideas. He talked to Verly who telephoned his neighbour with the result that although 'he'd never even heard of me' he was asked to go up to Woodway.

For a while John just rode work until such time as the Johnson-Houghtons were satisfied. Then he started riding for them in public. Following an odds-on winner with Gallant Welsh at Leicester in midsummer, he had an increasing number of rides and winners for his new stable. His final winning total for 1977 was thirty-three.

It was at this stage that Fulke told me that he was taking on John Reid. He said: 'I think he's very good indeed. But I'm not going to throw him in at the deep end when he's just out of his time. So he won't be first jockey. Lester and Willie will be riding some of them — and John will have the rest.' However, circumstances, John's own ability, and faulty judgment by Lester conspired to change all that.

There was at Woodway in 1977 a well-made brown two-year-old colt, superbly bred by Triple Crown hero Nijinsky out of the French Oaks winner Roselière and thus half-brother to the brilliant Rose Bowl. With the infinite patience that has always characterized the family, Fulke gave the backward colt all the time he demanded. At the back-end of 1977 John rode him in the Futurity at Doncaster. With his sensational low, sweeping action, Ile de Bourbon was still too immature and weak to handle the soft ground.

The following season 'the long fellow' jumped into the saddle. First time out on 4 May, One Thousand Guineas day at Newmarket, Ile de Bourbon challenged previously-raced Shirley Heights in the Heathorn Stakes and, in a hard finish, was beaten a short head. Not even Lester, who put up a pound overweight, could have foretold at this stage that the winner would triumph in two Derbys!

Twenty days later came the Predominate Stakes over 1½

miles at Goodwood. It has long appeared to me that Lester is always trying horses — asking them the stiffest possible questions to determine whether he will ride them again in the big races. If this is so, it is a major chink in his armour, which causes me to wonder whether he is really a horse-lover and makes me tremble for his future as a trainer. This was a perfect case in point.

Subsequent events proved that this was one of the strangest races ever run on the historic Sussex track. Fresh from his short-head Newmarket victory Shirley Heights had gone on to beat a very strong field for the Mecca-Dante Stakes at York. And he'd done it really well, being eased before the post.

His victims included such high-class colts as Julio Mariner, Sexton Blake and the Two Thousand Guineas runner-up, Remainder Man. He was obviously a very good classic colt indeed and, wherever he finished, Ile de Bourbon should be only inches away — well in front of all these other good classic candidates.

There was no Shirley Heights at Goodwood. Carson jumped the Queen's English Harbour off into the lead and made every inch of the running to win by 1½ lengths from Ile de Bourbon, who was receiving no less than 5 lb from his conqueror.

Fulke says: 'I think that he may still have been feeling the effects of that hard race at Newmarket. As long as he was having his own way in front, the Queen's English Harbour was a pretty good horse. Mind, our chap was still a bit backward. But I think Willie Carson pinched that race.'

It's easy to disappoint a horse and, perhaps Piggott, by never delivering an effective challenge to the leader, did just that. Or maybe this exceptionally intelligent colt took a dislike to the rider who had given him such a hard time first time out at Newmarket. Whatever the reason Lester discarded Ile de Bourbon. 'He decided he was no good,' says John.

Now we saw the immense advantage of having a retained jockey. On the Blewbury gallops John was really getting to know the Nijinsky colt, who was working most impressively and on 22 June they went to Royal Ascot for the 1½ mile King Edward VII Stakes.

Says Fulke: 'I'd told John Reid that I would only take him

off any of my horses for either Piggott or Carson. This time both were claimed — for Stradavinsky and Admiral's Launch respectively.'

As it turned out, this was the great chance, the turning-point in a young man's life. He never faltered.

Fulke continues: 'John got on so well with him, that he won very easily by 2½ lengths from Stradavinsky.'

Ile de Bourbon now had four owners: David McCall, former racing manager to the late Charles Engelhard who bred the colt, Sir Philip Oppenheimer, Mrs Helen Johnson-Houghton and her son, Fulke, the trainer.

After Royal Ascot the four owners decided to go for the big one over the same course and distance in a month's time — the £98,120 King George VI and Queen Elizabeth Diamond Stakes, so superbly sponsored by Sir Philip's firm, De Beers.

'I wasn't frightened', says Fulke, 'but I wasn't particularly confident of winning. I thought that the race was probably too soon and that Ile de Bourbon would be a better horse as a four-year-old. But I knew that John, who loved and understood him, would not knock him about or hurt him and I thought that he'd finish in the first three.'

Between races Ile de Bourbon continued to impress in his home-work at Blewbury, ridden either by John or his lad, William Reddy, son of old Bill Reddy, who was with Atty Persse. William had looked after the brown colt's sister, Rose Bowl.

The great day arrived. What a test for a young jockey, whose biggest success to date, apart from the King Edward VII, had been in a £6,000 handicap!

There was a truly international line-up for the big, glamorous event. Shirley Heights was unable to run again after the Irish Sweeps Derby. But he was more than adequately represented by Hawaiian Sound, whom he had beaten only inches at Epsom and at The Curragh, and by the Mullion challenger Exdirectory, who had divided them in the Irish classic and was perhaps unlucky not to have won.

Then there was the brilliant French Derby winner Acamas, running for Marcel Boussac and ridden by Yves Saint-Martin. Top French form was also represented by Trillion, Montcontour and Guadanius and Rex Magna. There was the much-travelled antipodean champion Balmerino and the Queen's

Dunfermline, winner the previous year of both the Oaks and the St Leger.

'I saddled Ile de Bourbon and watched the race with my wife on the trainers' stand,' says Fulke.

'After Hotgrove's Derby I never believe that my horse has won until he's actually past the post. But on this occasion I was pretty confident about a hundred yards before the straight.

'Sea Boat made the running for Dunfermline and they went such a blistering pace that my horse was the only one good enough to lay handy. When we moved up in Swinley Bottom and John kicked on, Yves Saint-Martin tried to go with him on Acamas. But he couldn't go the pace. The favourite was just not good enough.

'When Dunfermline took the lead, Ile de Bourbon went second and before the straight it was clear that she was tiring. We were going so easily, that it looked all over then.'

Ile de Bourbon swept into the lead after entering the straight and ran on strongly to win well by 1½ lengths from Acamas and Hawaiian Sound.

Far from losing anything by comparison with the finest international riders, John had 'ridden a blinder' with the cool, balanced judgment of a veteran. He had arrived. Now he is deservedly first jockey to Fulke Johnson-Houghton.

Despite the virus, which crippled the stable during 1978 after he and Ile de Bourbon had spreadeagled the field in the Coronation Cup over the Epsom Derby course, John finished the year with 72 winners.

II

The Jumping Game

David Nicholson has always found time to use his brain and forthright personality on behalf of jockeys, both when he was riding and now he is training. He takes after his admirable father, Frenchy, who has produced more top-class flat jockeys than even his one-time employer, Stanley Wootton.

Despite some adverse criticism of the new riding scheme whereby 'condition' jockeys may, like flat apprentices, ride for half fees, the trainer retaining the other half, David sticks to his guns.

'With the old set-up,' he says, 'the trainer could not afford to promote a National Hunt jockey who had never ridden. Except for a very few, there are no longer any true amateurs. So where are the leading jockeys of the future to come from, except Ireland?

'Over there they have all these "bumper" (amateur flat) races. And so many of the children hunt. They're all half made before they ever go racing. Add a flat apprenticeship and they're away.

'If a National Hunt trainer works for a realistic fee and pays proper wages, he must train horses and train young jockeys. And to promote a young N.H. jockey, the trainer must be prepared to send him anywhere at any time.

'This is one of the reasons why Alan Webb got going. He was prepared to drive and I was prepared to send him to Perth on Wednesday and Fontwell on Thursday for one outside ride at each meeting. As it happens, both won! This way the lad achieves connections, which, hopefully, will blossom.

'To promote a young jockey and really get him going, the trainer must not be selfish. He must allow outside people to use him. If there is a chance of a ride, the young jockey must bloody well go and ride it.

'He must be excused from "doing his two", mucking out,

riding out. It's awkward for the riding rota and for the head lad. But it's the only way a young man will ever get going.

'All this costs a lot of money these days. There must be some incentive to promote young jockeys. In the last few years there has been a grave shortage of N.H. jockeys. Most of the best young ones are Irish — Jonjo O'Neill, Tommy Carmody, John Burke and, in the recent past, champions Ron Barry and Tommy Stack.

'Three-quarters of the English trainers can't be bothered to try and make a jockey. They just sit, waiting for one to be made. Then they grab him. And as soon as things go wrong, they drop him.

'It so happens that these trainers, who are organizing the new scheme, all currently have excellent condition riders, whom we are promoting.

'Toby Balding has Brian Riley, and Josh Gifford has a whole host of them, including Richard Rowe, Hywel Davies and Christy Kinane. I have Alan Webb and Paul Carvill. And I'm happy to say that Alan has never stopped riding winners since he lost his claim.

'The boy must be really keen and so must the trainer. He must be dedicated, because it's hard enough to win races at the best of times.

'It's recommended in the *Racing Calendar* that the trainer is sent half the riding fees. He can do what he wants with it. He comes to an agreement with individual people. If a lad of 17 or 18 these days can't negotiate with his boss and vice versa, it's a bloody poor job. The trainer can give all the money back, if that is the agreement.

'We keep detailed weekly accounts for each person with a licence. Every Friday he reports to my accountant his expenses incurred during the week — valet, travelling, subsistence, overnight stay. When it's all worked out, in the long run there's nothing in it. All I am trying to do is to break even, have the satisfaction of making good jockeys and of having good riders on my horses.

'The critics say basically that the trainers should have nothing, that the system is being abused. I say that it's up to the condition jockey to be able to stand on his own two feet. If he feels hard done by, he can always go to the Jockeys' Association or the Trainers' Federation who are keeping a close eye on the operation of the system.

'In the old days amateurs used to go round for nothing to get the rides. If only we could have more National Hunt flat races, there would be greater opportunities to give backward horses and condition jockeys the experience they require.'

In fact I do not entirely agree with David when he more or less dismisses the amateur way in as practised so successfully in the past by the likes of Tim Brookshaw, Tim Molony, Stan Mellor, Dick Francis, Terry Biddlecombe, Bobby Beasley and Michael Scudamore, who all started their careers as 'Mr'.

Somerset farmer's son Richard Linley is improving all the time as Toby Balding's stable jockey, and Philip Blacker, who turned professional shortly before his twentieth birthday, has thoroughly earned his position as first jockey to Stan Mellor.

Moreover, in November 1979 David's own assistant trainer, 21-year-old Peter Scudamore followed in the footsteps of his father and turned professional just fifteen months after riding his first winner. Now a successful trainer, Michael was an outstanding horseman, who won the Grand National on Oxo and the Gold Cup on Linwell.

As a Cotswold neighbour of the Nicholsons, I have been particularly impressed with every aspect of young Peter as a strong stylist who, with ordinary luck, will soon be at the very top of the tree.

Thinking back to my own very moderate amateur riding days, I am reminded of a story told by the late Sandy Scratchley of the pre-war day when he was summoned by the stewards at a critical point of his riding career when he had been particularly successful.

'They asked to see my bank-pass book,' said Sandy. 'As the last entry was a hundred pounds from Aly Khan, I drew myself up to my full five feet plus and told them: "It's been a hard decision, gentlemen, but I've finally made up my mind to turn professional!"'

There was a time when I was deservedly hauled straight before the stewards, of whom the senior, now a General, had at one time been a top-class amateur rider. After delivering a well-earned rocket, he added: 'It's all right for you. You're doing this for fun. I had to ride for my bloody living!'

Some time later, over a drink, he told me that when, as a young cavalry officer, he won a big race before the war, and the happy owner asked him what he would like for a present, he would say how much he had long admired a certain gold cigarette-case in the window of a famous London jeweller. The owner would gladly order it to be sent to him. 'But as it just so happened that I already possessed an identical case', he said, 'the jeweller would kindly credit the sum to my account!'

Admittedly the system has been abused but, like everything else to do with National Hunt racing, amateur-riding is part of a British set-up which has no equal in any other country.

Of course, David's theories were right. We were back to the same situation as prevailed after the last war when Irish jockeys ruled the roost. In eight seasons Bryan Marshall, that superb horseman-jockey who, incidentally, served through the war as an officer in the Inniskilling Dragoon Guards, and Tim Molony, who was champion five times, equalling the record, held the leadership in the jockeys' table six times in five years, interrupted only by Fred Winter and Dick Francis. Martin Molony, too, the National Hunt connoisseur's dream jockey, had delighted us with his superb artistry.

Thereafter, however, England ruled the roost until the beginning of the seventies with Fred Winter, Tim Brookshaw, Stan Mellor, Josh Gifford, Terry Biddlecombe, Bob Davies and Graham Thorner. The only Irishman to ripple the English pond during these two decades was brilliant Bobby Beasley, champion of his country and one of the greatest of them all. It is worth noting also that until the seventies the champion jockeys were always based in the south or Midlands, never in the north.

Now the pendulum has swung back with a vengeance thanks to Irishmen Ron Barry, Tommy Stack, Jonjo O'Neill and Tommy Carmody — all of whom have earned their livings, for the most part, north of the Trent. With the exception of John Francome, their chief English rivals are already in their thirties.

Graham Thorner

Graham Thorner joined Tim Forster's stable at Letcombe Bassett straight from school in 1964 as a fifteen-year-old amateur. Two years later he rode his first winner, Longway, in a Newton Abbot hurdle race, turned professional the following season, was champion in 1971 and 1972, and stayed with Tim until his retirement in December 1979.

The tall, lean, polished trainer — a magnificent product of Eton and the 11th Hussars, who is so well versed in the ways of the country and of animals — and his energetic ultra-fit jockey were the perfect team. These two men greatly admire one another's dedication and professionalism. Forster says that he knew right from the start that Graham was destined to become a champion jockey.

'It was perfectly obvious from the beginning that he was going to be a fine rider,' he said. 'He immediately displayed natural ability, horsemanship and a racing brain. His outstanding asset was consistency.'

Graham counters: 'Very few men can get a horse just right for the job in hand better than Tim Forster. He's a fine trainer and a considerate employer. I knew only too well when I'd ridden a bad race, so Tim never bothered to mention it. I'd go over it again and again in my mind, sorting out what I could have done better, then we'd talk about it.'

Tim laughs. 'The video made quite a difference!' he says. 'Sometimes when I haven't been at the meeting where Graham has been riding, I'm greeted on his return home with "you made a proper nonsense of that third last fence." He would look at me, surprised. "I didn't," he'd say. "Want a bet? Come in and look at the television."'

Yes, they were a perfect team, as we saw in 1972 when they worked out a detailed plan together for Graham's riding of Tim's own horse Well To Do in the Grand National. Graham stuck to the plan with amazing accuracy throughout the four and a half miles of the Aintree chase and finished up winning by two lengths from Gay Trip, denying Terry Biddlecombe the ambition of a lifetime. In eight Grand Nationals Graham completed the course five times.

There is no finer judge than Tim who firmly contradicts the critics who claim that his jockey was too hard on his horses. Says Tim: 'My horses keep their form for long periods. This shows that they have a hard race only when absolutely necessary. And my owners were so fond of Graham that I had the devil's own job to persuade them to put anyone else up should I wish to run two horses in one race or have runners at more than one meeting.'

The son of a Somerset farmer, Graham is married to

Caroline Cooke, the daughter of an Oxfordshire farmer. With their four daughters they live in a Cotswold stone farmhouse near Cricklade with 42 acres, where Graham is constantly working to improve his stable yard and facilities.

I said earlier that reliability was his forte. He was always thereabouts in the first three of the jockeys' table and punters knew that they would invariably get a run for their money with Thorner.

Jeff King

It is no accident that two of England's finest riders are associated with Bob Turnell. A fine, thinking jockey with lovely hands, Bob rode a lot of winners for the late Lord Bicester and for Ivor Anthony. The son of a horse-dealer from Towcester, he set up a small stable at Chipping Sodbury after he had given up race-riding. Then he moved to his present quarters at Ogbourne near Marlborough.

Devonian Jeff King was born at Shaldon near Teignmouth in 1941. He always wanted to be a jockey and was lucky to have been born in such a sporting county. He was lucky too to catch the eye of Miss Frances Stanbury, whose mare Dreamboat won the first Foxhunter jumping event then staged at Harringay. She schooled young Jeff well, so that he enjoyed considerable success both in the hunting field with his local pack, the Silverton, and in juvenile show-jumping classes.

So well did he perform in those early days that he was spotted by Major Faudel Philips, a very successful producer of show hacks and founder of the Pony Club. It was he who arranged that Jeff should be apprenticed to Sir Gordon Richards at Ogbourne soon after his fifteenth birthday.

Jeff then weighed six and a half stone. However, when his apprenticeship ended three years later, he had built up to over eight stone which effectively prevented any chance of success on the flat.

So, still determined to be a successful jockey, he realized that he would have to turn to jumping and made the short move down the road to Bob Turnell at the beginning of the 1959-60 season.

His first ride after joining Bob was Panda in a four-year-old hurdle at Stratford in January 1960. Although he finished out of the money on that occasion, he rode his first winner less than a month later, Pilgrim Father, trained by Ben Leigh, on whom he won a selling hurdle by four lengths at Warwick. He rode three more winners that season, bringing his score to four victories out of twelve rides. Since then Jeff has averaged forty winners in a season and in 1971-72, when he rode as joint first jockey with Johnny Haine to Bob Turnell, he scored his highest total of sixty-six.

That was his last season as stable-jockey, because inevitably the trainer's talented son Andy was now fit to take the job over. It had been a good partnership and established a friendship between Bob and Jeff which has remained steady and constant ever since.

Looking back on this period I remember vividly the immense satisfaction I derived from the sympathetic partnership between Jeff and one of the best horses he ever rode, The Laird, a big brown whose ability and temperament were not quite matched by his courage and resolution. Somehow Jeff managed to give him confidence.

I shall never forget how near this confidence came to sensational triumph in the 1968 Cheltenham Gold Cup, the race which Jeff would most like to win. It was the year that was expected to produce the thrill of Arkle's return, fifteen months after his tragic accident at Kempton.

Unhappily it was not to be and Fort Leney substituted for his great stable-companion. Three years earlier in the National Hunt Handicap Chase on the opening day of the same meeting, the bay Fortina gelding, then only seven years old, had strained a heart valve as, conceding lumps of weight, he was narrowly beaten by Bob Turnell's candidate, Rondetto, another of Jeff's favourite horses, ridden on this occasion by Johnny Haine.

Fort Leney was given a complete rest the following year. He came back the next season to win three races, and was now fresh from scoring Tom Dreaper's seventh consecutive victory in that famous trial, the Leopardstown Chase. After every race he was given a check-up by a human-heart specialist who had treated him successfully throughout. He had the invaluable assistance of Pat Taaffe.

Mill House, free now of the fear of Arkle, was in the field along with that other top-class staying chaser, little grey

Stalbridge Colonist. Overnight rain had eased the going, and a fine day, excellent racing and a bumper Tote jackpot had attracted an enormous crowd. Two punters, who nominated all six winners, each collected £55,927 from a record pool over the sticks.

As Mill House, looking superb, set off in front and made the running for the first circuit, jumping with all his old fluency, it seemed that Fulke Walwyn's care and patience would be rewarded. But this time the old champion was not allowed to have matters his own way. Arkle had taught his jockey how to beat 'the big horse'. So Taaffe and Fort Leney stuck tenaciously to him and, as they started up for the last time, Mill House was changing legs. Upsides with his Irish rival at the open ditch after the water, he hit the fence and came down. They must have heard the crowd's disappointed gasp in Birmingham!

All this time Jeff had been nursing The Laird, hunting him round, inspiring the confidence which he so urgently needed for the supreme test ahead. Now, as Fort Leney went on, The Laird closed with him, closely followed by Stalbridge Colonist, and the battle was on. At the third from home, the famous Joel 'black, red cap' went into the lead, but Fort Leney struggled back on terms and three horses were almost together at the second last, where Stalbridge Colonist, under pressure, made a mistake which probably cost him the race.

Pat drove Fort Leney back into the lead over the last, but Jeff was not beaten yet. Undismayed by this great jockey and his brave horse, he rode the finish of a lifetime up the hill and failed by only a neck to catch Fort Leney, who came back to frenzied Irish cheers of 'good old Tom' for Dreaper, whose first words were: 'There's nothing wrong with this chap's heart now.' But the English pair who had given their hearts, their all, were forgotten.

But Jeff himself, whose other successes on The Laird included the Massey Fergusson Gold Cup and Cathcart Challenge Cup, both at Cheltenham, will never be forgotten. When a man is regarded universally by his fellow jockeys as the greatest of his time, there is no argument.

I mentioned Rondetto. This was the splendid horse on whom Jeff won the Hennessey Gold Cup and the Stones Ginger Wine Chase and who was thirteen when he rode him into third place behind Highland Wedding and Steel Bridge in the 1969 Grand National. He was a really tough, genuine customer with the same terrier-like qualities as his rider, who still has no equal over the last three fences.

Jeff's other big race winners have included Dormant (King George VI Chase), Red Tide (Topham Trophy), Money Market (Anthony Mildmay, Peter Cazelet Memorial Trophy), Tudor Dance (Cheltenham Grand Annual), Otter Way (Whitbread Gold Cup), Indianapolis (Schweppes Gold Trophy), Flash Imp (Imperial Cup) and Canasta Lad (Arkle Trophy). He has also won races at Baden-Baden in Germany and Murano in Italy on Octavo and a Norwegian Grand National on Josh Gifford's Avondhu.

Apart from the normal periods of concussion, broken collar bones, etc., which are part and parcel of a jumping jockey's life, Jeff has suffered only three serious breakages: skull, pelvis and, at the end of 1978, his right leg.

Blunt and outspoken, he does not suffer fools gladly. But Jeff is exceptionally kind, unselfish and public-spirited. He never fails to turn out for charity cricket matches, donkey derbys and show-jumping events. I can vouch for the fact that he is almost as good and stylish over the show fences as over the black ones.

Jeff lives with his wife, Maureen, and two children, David and Elizabeth, at Broad Hinton with a clear view south to the downs which overlook Ogbourne where he has spent so much of his life. He already has twenty-two boxes and forty acres. It will be a sad day for all of us when Jeff retires. But he will not be lost to racing. He will make an excellent trainer.

Andy Turnell

Those who bemoan the fact that British racing has become devoid of characters should look again at the jumping scene. Individualists — those men with the strength of their convictions — are still in abundance in the National Hunt world and, in the seventies, we were confronted with a new-style star in the tall, slim shape of Andy Turnell who has developed his own unique style of riding over fences and hurdles.

The first jump jockey to adopt the short leather and exaggerated crouch was George Duller, who rode so many winners over hurdles in the late twenties and early thirties.

Readers will by now have appreciated that I deplore the indiscriminate use of ultra-short stirrup leathers as practised by the British flat-race jockeys of today. There is a big difference between these little men and their jumping counterparts, Terry Biddlecombe and Andy Turnell, who have adjusted the length of their stirrups to the occasion and to the individual horse.

Terry, of course, has retired. He, like his brother-in-law, Bob Davies, was one of the stars of my book, *Steeplechase Jockeys: The Great Ones*. But Andy is happily still with us and a glance at his list of big race triumphs will convince anyone that here is an outstanding rider of the highest class.

You had to be very good to ride as first jockey to Ivor Anthony. Bob Turnell did so with conspicuous success for many years. So an outstanding jockey became an outstanding trainer when he took out his first licence in 1954, six years after the birth of his twin sons, Andrew and Robert.

'I wasn't all that keen on riding at the age of two or three', says Andy, 'but from four onwards it was the only thing that mattered. I hunted a lot and took part in all the usual Pony Club activities.' His father had always been a keen hunting man and has brought many good horses like The Laird back to winning form with a few happy days following hounds.

Apprenticed to Bob, Andy rode his first winner on the flat at Worcester three weeks before his fifteenth birthday. 'I only rode about a dozen winners on the flat', he says, 'before I got too heavy and started to ride jumping.'

But Bob was wise, even hard, on his son. There was no question of giving him favours or plunging him in at the deep end. As far as the Ogbourne stable was concerned, the jockeys were Jeff King and Johnny Haine. Andy had the left-overs and otherwise had to make his own way.

Nevertheless, these left-overs were well chosen by Bob, who, with the help of such splendid owners as Jim Joel and his cousin, the late Mrs John Rogerson, was quietly building his son's confidence, widening his experience and giving him a sound, solid introduction to his future career.

So Andy, at the age of sixteen, was quickly running through his apprentice allowance and making a name for himself through horses like Mayfair Bill, on whom he won the County Handicap Hurdle at the National Hunt Festival,

Sky Pink, Flash Bulb and Black King. That season he scored a double on the last two at Lingfield. He won three races each on Sky Pink and Mayfair Bill, with the result that he soon became recognised and admired by the racing fraternity.

Then, in 1972, luck, which is always an essential ingredient of racing success, took a hand. Andy says: 'I wouldn't have been first jockey to my father then if Johnny Haine hadn't gone to Toby Balding. Jeff King looked to have a good retainer with Peter Bailey. So at Christmas father told me that Johnny would be first jockey and I would be second. Within a month, however, Johnny had gone to Toby and there I was, stable-jockey.'

Two years earlier Andy had married Kathyrine Smith, daughter of a well-known hunting family and a good point-to-point rider. Her father, Tom Smith, manages one of the Duke of Beaufort's farms, breeds some useful horses and trains a few on a permit. One of his brothers, Arthur, bred Cuckolder, who might yet win a National for Andy. The other, John, is the father of Richard Smith, who was forced to retire from the saddle following a crashing fall at Newton Abbot in which he severely damaged his neck. Andy and Kathyrine have two children. They still like to hunt whenever they get a chance, but opportunities are somewhat limited now.

Of course, Andy's ultra-short stirrup leathers, even over fences, are the chief talking point. He sits as tight as a limpet, going with his horse, never jabbing it in the mouth. He has beautiful hands and perfect balance.

I asked him why he adopted this style. He said: 'When I was riding some winners for Frank Cundell while Johnny Cook was hurt, I had a painful knock on the inside of my knee and, to avoid hurting it on the saddle, I pulled my leathers right up. I found I was much more comfortable and that it really works with all decent racehorses. They seem to run better for you when you are slightly forward of the point of balance.

'I have always considered that riding under National Hunt rules was no different from the flat, except that there were obstacles in the way, and that if you could stay on board you should adopt the same style.

'I admit I fall off sometimes, perhaps four times in a season, about the same as other jockeys, but not because of my short leathers. I use my balance and grip with my ankles. If a horse "misses one out" I just keep my bum down and my hands low on his neck. My father was shocked when I started to ride like this, but the style suits me and it produced results, so he's had to accept it.

'Mind you, I don't think people realize that I adjust my "jerk" a lot as I'm cantering down. I'll ride much longer on the kind of horse you get at the bad jumping meetings, which needs more brute force than jockeyship; or on a little green, duck-hearted three-year-old, who might run out if I hadn't my legs to keep it in. I also keep my leathers longer when I'm riding one of those old three-mile chasers where your only chance, when he's stone-cold, is to sit down and boot him.'

So speaks a true horseman. Andy continued: 'Riding very short is much better when your horse falls. Nine times out of ten you are catapulted clear. If you're riding longer and sitting too tight, sort of glued to the saddle, you can get well and truly buried like poor Bill Rees on Dunkirk.'

Bad falls can reduce geniuses of the saddle to limping has-beens in a painfully quick process. Andy is quite realistic: 'So far, touching wood,' he says, 'I've been very lucky. I've broken my collar-bone three times and I've hurt my back twice.' This is an amazingly short list of injuries in view of the fact that he is so often perched high in the saddle, like Lester Piggott, and relies on the same sense of perfect balance to keep himself there.

In fact his poise looks so precarious that an uninitiated bookmaker would surely make Andy Turnell odds-on to come down at the first — and the informed punter would just as surely clean-up. For Turnell, again like Piggott, has flouted convention. And whilst he may never get the sort of following that is commanded by our greatest practising jockey, he is, indisputably, jumping's answer to Lester.

John Francome

If timing were the name of the game, there would be just one British champion jockey, John Francome, who was born on 13 December 1952.

This son of a Swindon builder had taken no interest at all

in racing and had not even heard of Fred Winter when he was taken on for a two weeks' trial at Lambourn late in 1969. He admits that he had not even seen a race on television.

However there are other branches of the horse world apart from racing and, from the age of four, John Francome had thought of little else than riding ponies. He was given his first pony when he was seven and did well in local shows and gymkhanas. His second pony, Tranzy, was a star, who won three first prizes, two seconds and a third at Marlborough Show in 1963 and carried his young rider in the finals of the Prince Philip Games at the Horse of the Year Show at Wembley, representing the VWH team. This is the splendid event which invariably steals the show for television viewers of Wembley.

After Tranzy's successes John's father, Norman Francome, gave him a strawberry roan called Red Paul. On this horse he was good enough to represent Britain in the International Show Jumping event in the summer of 1969 when the team finished fourth at Dinard. The following year when on holiday from Fred Winter's, he was a member of the team which included Anne Coleman, daughter of the television sports commentator David Coleman, that won the event for Britain at St Moritz. John also won the Young Riders' Jumping Championship at Hickstead in 1970.

However, by 1969, John had realized that it was time to decide whether or not to make show-jumping his career. This decision was taken out of his hands somewhat by Willie Cosgrove, a part-time labourer in Norman Francome's building firm, who occasionally rode out for Fred Winter. It was Willie who suggested that John should approach Fred with the idea of working for him and possibly becoming a jockey.

Although the greatest champion jockey of them all worried initially that John might put on too much weight because he had such large hands and feet, he took him on trial for a few weeks. This decision was fully justified when, in his first ride in public, eleven days before his eighteenth birthday on 2 December 1970, John won a three-mile hurdle at Worcester on Multigrey. He finished up that season with four winners, boosted that total to nineteen the following season, and scored twenty-one, thirty-one and seventy in successive seasons before finishing up as Champion Jockey with ninety-six in 1975-76.

Richard Pitman, John's mentor and guide in those early days with Fred Winter, wrote a book entitled *Good Horses Make Good Jockeys*. This has been, of course, undoubtedly true as regards Francome too, because Fred Winter invariably through a season produces some of the best jumpers in the world in superlative condition. Enough to make any jockey a good one!

Perhaps one could say that about John's Gold Cup victory on Midnight Court. Nevertheless there is no doubt that he can ride some quite exceptional races, going the shortest way and always, as I say, showing an incredible gift for 'seeing a stride'. I always thought that Stan Mellor was the best, but, having seen Francome judging his fences from such a long way away, I have my doubts now.

He is particularly good through a race, but suffers in a finish compared with some of the jockeys I have written about here. I just wish that John was as consistent as his guv'nor used to be. But I can state without fear of contradiction that when he is good he's very, very good . . . .

Steve Smith-Eccles

Fred Winter's success with the former junior show-jumping champion has been more than matched by Tom Jones's production of Steve Smith-Eccles who, despite his double-barrelled name, is the son of a proud Derbyshire miner with nearly forty years' underground service to his credit.

Witty, intelligent Steve, full of the bounce and drive that are so essential in a successful jockey, came to Newmarket at the age of sixteen straight from grammar school. He had one ride in public before increasing weight finished any idea of a flat career. Then Tom, one of the brainiest and most knowledgeable trainers in the business, brought his protégé along slowly like a good horse.

'There were two things about Stephen,' he says. 'First, that he pestered the life out of me to get a chance. Second, that when he got it, he seemed to know exactly what to do. When schooling, he always did the right thing, and on the racecourse he immediately had the natural, race-riding gift of dropping himself into the position he wanted and letting the rest get in each other's way. That's very exceptional.'

There followed experience, experience and more experience: schooling; riding work, and moderate rides in races. There were the inevitable falls and a few winners until the 1977-78 season when Steve was twenty-two years old. Ian Watkinson left Tom to ride for Peter Bailey and thus provided the opportunity for the strongly-made, 5 ft 6 in. young man to become stable-jockey.

Tom's particularly bold act of faith was rewarded. Steve rode fifty-one winners that season. There were some big thrills in that total, starting when the old American jumping phenomenon, Tingle Creek, broke the two-mile track record at Sandown. Swift Shadow won the Marlow Ropes John Skeaping Hurdle on the same course and then at Cheltenham's National Hunt Festival, Sweet Joe won the Sun Alliance Chase.

A number of heavy falls, including one at Devon and Exeter in March 1979 when Master Wrekin tripped up over a fallen hurdle, breaking his rider's neck, have proved Steve's toughness. But this is by no means the only quality that makes the popular miner's son such a splendid prospect.

Says Tom Jones: 'For a start, Stephen is always controlled and perfectly balanced on his horses, which is what helps them jump. People who say he's been winning on all sorts of moderate horses by just being a tough egg have got the analysis upside down. He's been successful on these horses for precisely the opposite reason. Instead of getting shoved and pushed from start to finish by some mindless muscle-man, they've been given a really cool, well-judged race. For me Stephen is a natural to be champion. I'm only surprised he isn't already.'

Tom switched his interests mainly to the flat at the same time as leading amateur rider Nicky Henderson left Fred Winter, to whom he had been assistant trainer, and started up on his own. He signed Steve Smith-Eccles as stable-jockey to his Lambourn stable. The result has been so successful that, as I write, Steve is second on the list. In my mind there is not much doubt that Tom's prophecy will be fulfilled in the near future. Steve looks sure to be champion jockey.

12

Those Irishmen

Northern-based Irishmen have given a new look to British National Hunt racing in the seventies. Of course, in 1974 we were treated to an exhibition of all-time greatness when Bobby Beasley came back from oblivion to win the Cheltenham Gold Cup on Captain Christy. But the jockeys who concerned us most in the seventies learnt, like Bobby, on the flat and are exceptional performers over obstacles.

Ron Barry

By coincidence, the first of them, Ron Barry, was Beasley's victim in that epic race, when he was attempting a repeat Gold Cup victory with The Dikler for Fulke Walwyn.

Ron was born in Limerick in 1943. Riding from an early age, he was small enough to be apprenticed on the flat. It is hard now to imagine 'big Ron' as a tiny apprentice with Anne Biddle and her private trainer Tommy Shaw. 'When I had my first ride on The Curragh', Ron says, 'I weighed just 6 st 5 lbs in colours. I was seventeen years old then.'

He rode his first winner on the level at Gowran Park but he was soon shooting up in height and inevitably putting on weight as he grew older. He decided to transfer his attention to jumping and with that aim came over to Britain in 1964, attaching himself to Wilf Crawford's small stable in Scotland.

19 October 1964 at Ayr was an eventful day. Riding four-year-old Silken Su in the first division of the novice hurdle, Ron had a bad time of it at the start and finished tailed off.

In the following event, the Punchbowl Handicap Hurdle, Hamilcar was up with the leader at the first hurdle where he unshipped his rider. But three races later Final Approach gave

Ron his first winner over obstacles, making all the running to win by twelve lengths from his veteran compatriot Pat Buckley.

At the end of the following season he could claim only 3 lbs and in October 1966 he lost the allowance altogether. Now the best judges in the north recognized him as a powerful fearless rider through a race and in a finish. By 1968-69 he was on the jockeys' list, joint ninth with Jeff King and Roy Edwards on thirty-five winners apiece. The following season he moved up to seventh with forty-four winners, equal to Brian Fletcher and Graham Thorner. He was on his way.

He had struck up a grand partnership with Gordon Richards, for whom he was to ride such excellent horses as Titus Oates. 'And I've been with G.W.R. virtually ever since,' says Ron proudly. In 1974 he married his lovely wife, Liz, with whom he lives at Pooley Bridge, near Penrith, handy for Gordon Richards' stables.

Southern trainers were not slow to appreciate Ron's potential and he enjoyed considerable success with Fulke Walwyn, who said to me: 'He's my type of chap!' Praise indeed from the maestro. It was for Fulke that Ron won the Cheltenham Gold Cup of 1973 on The Dikler.

Ron had suddenly rocketed to fame in the 1972-73 season, not only finishing as champion jockey but breaking the all-time record number of winners with 125.

As though that were not enough, he has twice shown the rest of the world what a first-class horseman and jockey he is by crossing the Atlantic to win the Colonial Cup in South Carolina on Grand Canyon.

Tommy Stack

Kerry-born Thomas Brendan Stack is two years younger than Ron Barry. I asked Tommy how he came into the bloodstock industry in the first place and learnt with interest that he had long enjoyed a stud background. After leaving his Jesuit school at 17½, he spent eighteen months with a Dublin insurance firm. 'I'd ridden ponies, messing about at home', he says, 'but I'd had very little hunting and didn't know much about horses when I grew sick of office life. I backed a million to one chance and applied for a job with Bobby

Renton.' That million to one chance came off. The famous old northern trainer, who was riding winners himself at the age of 70, agreed to take on the young Irishman.

'When the butler met me off the plane,' Tommy recalled, 'I knew nobody in racing.'

Bobby Renton had never 'made' a jockey before, but this one was a natural. 'Within two months I had my first ride and finished second on New Money. A month later at Wetherby on 2 October I won on the same horse. My first winner. If it hadn't worked out like that I'd have almost certainly been back in Kerry dairy-farming with my family.'

But the fairy-tale did come true in a way surprisingly reminiscent of Vincent O'Brien's training career. Tommy's first ride over fences was neither at Sedgefield, Fakenham, Cartmel or Mulingar. It was at Cheltenham, headquarters of Britain's great sport. And Well Packed, ridden by amateur Mr T. Stack, came up the famous hill and passed the winning post in front.

He never looked back. After two years as an amateur and eleven as a professional, he had been champion twice and won the Grand National on Red Rum. His personality and intelligence made him universally popular in the toughest of all schools — the National Hunt weighing room.

'But everything has to come to an end,' he philosophizes. 'With me it was the last time that Red Rum ever ran, at Haydock on 1 March 1978. This was just my one really bad accident. I broke my pelvis and that was it.'

For many years Tommy had been a close friend of John Magnier, now managing director of the famous Coolmore/Castle Hyde Stud complex in Ireland. 'All the time I was riding I owned five or six mares and invested in stallion shares,' he says. 'John looked after the mares for me.'

'I was lucky enough to start off on the right foot by breeding Brook, winner of the Hungerford Stakes at Newbury, and now, owned by Dr Carlo (Grundy) Vittadini, leading first season sire in Italy. I bought her dam, carrying him, and later sold her to Robert Sangster.'

So when he was offered the job as manager of Longfield Stud, the Cashel, Tipperary outpost of Coolmore, the transition was quite simple and the casting was absolutely ideal. Tommy and Liz have settled down superbly in their home which was once owned by Vincent O'Brien, who lives close by at Ballydoyle. When last in Ireland, I spoke to Vincent of the new Longfield Stud manager.

'I would think that Tommy is brilliant,' said the maestro. 'He's a perfectionist and is making a lot of improvements. A tremendous worker.'

Jonjo O'Neill

Records are made to be broken and, while it was surprising to find Ron Barry's record of 125 shattered so quickly, it was not so surprising to find that the new record-breaker was Jonjo O'Neill to whom 'big Ron' has been mentor and guide since his arrival in England.

John Joseph O'Neill was one of four sons born to Tom O'Neill, a grocer, in Castletownroche, Co. Cork. I like the story of how he came by his first pony. Although he was mad on horses from the start, there was not enough money in the family to buy him a mount. His determination to achieve this aim still characterizes Jonjo today.

Originally, as a boy, when he was delivering groceries around the Cork roads on a bicycle belonging to the shop, his only chance to ride came when a neighbouring farmer lent him a pony and trap. Jonjo was supposed to take the pony to the pump for a drink, but, after that, he would drive to the field, slip off the harness and ride the pony bareback.

By delivering groceries and running messages on the bike, he managed to save up £7 and spent the money on two piglets, whom he treated as pets and sold when fattened up for £32. With that cash in hand he went out and bought a pony called Dolly for £27!

He served a three-year apprenticeship at The Curragh with Mick Connolly for whom he rode three winners: one on the flat, one over hurdles and the other over fences.

After a period of traumatic indecision during 1972, when he first came over to Gordon W. Richards, Jonjo returned disappointed to Ireland and then came back to Greystoke again, and made good. His first four rides in England on his return all won and he went on to finish with thirty-eight winners by the end of the season. Stable-jockey Ron Barry was a tremendous help and they formed a lasting friendship.

In 1974 he won the Stone's Ginger Wine Chase on Erring

Burn, and the Topham Trophy at Aintree on Clear Cut. But the horse with whom Jonjo will always be associated is everyone's favourite, Sea Pigeon, whom he has ridden with such sympathetic brilliance to win the highest class races both over hurdles and on the flat. Two bad accidents have marred his career: in 1975 and in his first season as reigning champion jockey.

What a time he had had in 1977-78 when he finished with that unprecedented 149 winners! He had been placed first, second or third in 300 of his 545 races. He had a winning percentage of 27.33, producing a level stakes profit of £95.63. Only one other rider in the top twenty could show any profit at all on his total number of rides, and several others were minus as much as O'Neill won. He is forceful over fences, a fine judge and particularly powerful in a finish. He is shy, charming and immensely popular.

There were two meetings on that final day of the jump season in June 1978. If the aeroplane due to take Jonjo from Stratford-on-Avon to Market Rasen had been on time, he would have achieved the incredible target of 150 winners. As it was, he had beaten the old record by twenty-four and had ridden no fewer than five winners in an afternoon on 19 April.

Tommy Carmody

Still up in the north, the Dickinson success story is a family affair, run by father Tony, mother Monica and son Michael. Trained originally by the maestro, Frenchy Nicholson, ultra-tall Michael was an outstanding jockey through a race, showing an exceptional degree of intelligence and balance until injury forced him to retire from the saddle.

Personal recommendation and observation persuaded the Dickinsons to take on Tommy Carmody to fill Michael's shoes as stable-jockey and they have never regretted it since.

Like Ron Barry, Tommy comes from Limerick. One of eight children of a machine manufacturer, he was riding in gymkhanas and pony races from his earliest years.

Liam Browne, the former jockey — who, as a trainer at The Curragh, is fast earning a reputation as the Frenchy Nicholson of Ireland — spotted the boy and apprenticed him when he was fourteen. Tommy's first winner was at Sligo and, in a matter of three seasons, he had established himself as one of the best young riders in his country. He was champion apprentice three times and placed in six classics before weight forced him into the jumping game. He was no stranger to England because he had already won on Mr Kildare and Hilly Way at Cheltenham. Nevertheless, his meteoric start with the Dickinsons was little short of incredible. His first winner for them, I'm A Driver, was in a novice chase at Ayr on 14 October. In the next fortnight of that 1978-79 season, he rode seventeen more winners and earned the Bolinger 'Jockey of the Month' award in December.

His big race successes included I'm A Driver in the Buchanan Whisky Gold Cup and the King George VI Chase on Gay Spartan. The two jockeys Tommy admires most are Ron Barry and Andy Turnell whom he finds great professionals and particularly hard to beat.

Although he started late, Tommy finished that first season with seventy-one winners, which took him to second in the jockeys' championship list behind John Francome and ahead of Bob Davies and Jonjo O'Neill. Certainly Jonjo had done particularly well after his crippling injury early on. But young Carmody's superb style, elegance, balanced judgment and flat-race finishing have already earned him the highest praise from some of the finest judges, who are already saying that he is a second Martin Molony. That is truly praise indeed.

Index